COMMUTER SPOUSES

COMMUTER SPOUSES

New Families in a Changing World

DANIELLE J. LINDEMANN

ILR PRESS
AN IMPRINT OF
CORNELL UNIVERSITY PRESS
ITHACA AND LONDON

First published 2019 by Cornell University Press

Printed in the United States of America

Library of Congress Cataloging-in-Publication Data

Names: Lindemann, Danielle J., author.
Title: Commuter spouses : new families in a changing world / Danielle J. Lindemann.
Description: Ithaca [New York] : ILR Press, an imprint of Cornell University Press, 2019. | Includes bibliographical references and index.
Identifiers: LCCN 2018041026 (print) | LCCN 2018042392 (ebook) | ISBN 9781501731198 (e-book pdf) | ISBN 9781501731204 (e-book epub/mobi) | ISBN 9781501731181 | ISBN 9781501731181 (pbk. ; alk. paper)
Subjects: LCSH: Commuter marriage—United States. | Work and family—United States. | Long-distance relationships—United States.
Classification: LCC HQ734 (ebook) | LCC HQ734 .L5667 2019 (print) | DDC 306.3/6—dc23
LC record available at https://lccn.loc.gov/2018041026

For Hunter. YMB.

Contents

Acknowledgments   ix

Introduction   1

1. Apart Together: Individualism, Interdependence, and the Meaning of (Commuter) Marriage   16

2. Virtually Together: Space, Place, and Communication Technologies   34

3. Nobody's Decision: The "Choice" to Live Apart   58

4. "They Don't Have to Pick up Their Husbands' Shoes": Doing and Undoing Gender   78

5. Who Benefits from (Commuter) Marriage?   98

6. "But Are They Happy?"   116

Conclusion   126

Appendix A: Methodological Appendix   141

Appendix B: Interview Schedule   148

Appendix C: Follow-up Survey   153

Notes   157

References   163

Index   179

ACKNOWLEDGMENTS

Whenever I present this research at conferences and I get to my "Acknowledgments" slide, the laughably sprawling text is a testament to my own journey attempting to reconcile family and geography while seeking permanent work.

When I first began this project in 2011, I was a postdoctoral research scholar at Vanderbilt University's Curb Center for Art, Enterprise, and Public Policy. There were a number of individuals there—including Steven Tepper, Dan Cornfield, and Elizabeth Long Lingo—who provided feedback and support as I got the study up and running.

At the conclusion of my fellowship, I accepted a job as research director of the Center for Women and Work at Rutgers University—a move that got me back living with my husband again, albeit with a long commute. There I finished conducting the interviews for the project and began data analysis, with support and advice from multiple individuals, including Dana Britton, Terri Boyer, Karen Cerulo, and Pat Roos. The Rutgers University Research Council provided funding for some of the interview transcriptions. While at Rutgers, I also gave birth to my daughter, Fiona. She gets a "thank you" here for being the light of my life and all around fantastic.

In 2015, I began a job as a professor at Lehigh University—a move that now has me living with my husband and child "permanently" (contingent on tenure!), albeit with an even longer commute. As I made the final push on the book, I received not only support from my colleagues in the Department of Sociology and Anthropology, but also funding in the form of Lehigh's Paul J. Franz Award.

Some material from this book has appeared previously in other venues. Some parts of chapter 2 were published in an article I wrote for *Contexts* (Lindemann 2017a), and some material from chapter 1 has appeared in the *Journal of Marriage and Family* (Lindemann 2017b). Elements of chapter 4 have appeared in an article in *Sex Roles* (Lindemann 2017c). I would like to thank the two anonymous reviewers for Cornell University Press, as well as the additional anonymous scholars who provided feedback for these other journal articles. They have helped me to strengthen the work substantially. Fran Benson at Cornell has my gratitude for believing in this book and helping to move it along through the review process. I would also like to thank Marta Murray-Close and Mary Holmes for generously sharing their own research on this topic with me.

I would be remiss in not thanking the people in my personal life who were supports for me through the writing of this book. That list is lengthy but includes my husband, Hunter, my mother, Louise, our superhero, Alyssa, and my best friend, Jess. I'd also like to thank Shaina for her much-needed cerebral rejuvenation breaks, mainly involving episodes of reality TV shows.

Finally, and most important, it is crucial for me to acknowledge all of the commuter spouses who spoke to me for this project. I use pseudonyms for all participants in the book and therefore cannot mention them by name, but they have my heartfelt gratitude. Without their willingness to take time away from their hectic schedules and open up their lives to me, this book would not exist.

Commuter Spouses

INTRODUCTION

In early September of 2011, I touched down in Nashville with the sunburn from my honeymoon still tingling like a fresh tattoo on my back. It sounds like a lyric from a country music song, but it was my life. I was moving for a new job—a postdoctoral fellowship at Vanderbilt University. My husband, an attorney in New York City who had recently made partner at his firm, would continue to live in our Brooklyn apartment. We would do this for two years.

This book is about people who have done what I did: lived apart from their husbands or wives in service to their dual professional careers. Some researchers estimate that a growing number of married Americans are now living apart from their spouses.[1] The lifestyle has become popular enough to spawn self-help books with titles like *Super Commuter Couples: Staying Together When a Job Keeps You Apart* (Bearce 2013) and *The Commuter Marriage: Keep Your Relationship Close While You're Far Apart*—the latter promising that it "will help you keep your relationship connected when you're disconnected" (Tessina 2008, xviii).

More broadly, the public has had a fascination with long-distance love and the role of individuality within intimate relationships. Journalists have picked up on this theme. "Divided We Stand," reports one *Telegraph* article on couples who do not live together (Neustatter 2013). The title of one *New York Times* piece, "Home Alone Together," perches on the page atop photos of two halves of a couple, gazing smilingly toward each other from their separate residences (Brooke 2006). Another piece, in the *New York Times* Real Estate section, explores how this phenomenon relates to the contemporary housing crisis (Rosenblum 2013). Researchers such as Robert Putnam (2000), Eric Klinenberg (2012), and Susan Cain (2013) have detailed the appeal of spending time alone, and examples of non-cohabitating spouses have dotted the cultural landscape. For instance, the actress Amy Poehler and her then-husband Will Arnett lived on separate coasts filming their respective television shows for several years of their marriage. The politician Ted Cruz and his wife Heidi, too, lived apart for several years while he was Texas's solicitor general and she worked at the Treasury Department in Washington, DC (Harlan 2016).

These atypical marital arrangements make for interesting journalism. Yet they are also important on a broader sociological level, for reasons beyond the nuances of managing a two-residence marriage. In fact, "commuter spouses" have evolved out of major transitions in the meaning and structure of work, gender, and families—and they sit in a unique position to shed light on the social dynamics that have shaped their marriages.

An Illuminating Population

Though it explores multiple themes, this book coalesces around a central question: how can this seemingly liminal population shed light on large-scale shifts in the dynamics of marriage, family, gender roles, and professional careers? In the chapters that follow, I present my findings from ninety-seven in-depth interviews with current or former commuter spouses (for information about the sampling process and sample characteristics, as well as data collection and analysis, see appendix A). I argue that these commuters, seemingly atypical in their lifestyles, reflect and embody (and, yes, sometimes disrupt) large-scale developments in the ways we think about gender and marriage, in the ways we communicate, in the ways we conceptualize labor, and in the ways we reconcile work and family. By observing an extreme result of these changes—couples who physically separate in order to make their professional lives work—we can better understand these historical dynamics. But at the same time that noncohabitating spouses can help us learn about change, they also shed light on the durability of some cultural ideals, even within these seemingly nonnormative relationships.

In the early 1980s, sociologists Naomi Gerstel and Harriet Engel Gross noted that researchers had attributed the commuter marriage to four factors: an increasing societal emphasis on individualism; tighter, more competitive job markets (Gerstel 1977); married women's increasing participation in the professions (Gerstel 1977; Gross 1980a; Kirschner and Walum 1978); and greater gender equality within marriage (Gross 1980a; Gerstel 1978).

In the decades since Gerstel and Gross first wrote about this topic, we have seen an extension of these developments. For example, researchers have found persistent trends toward individualization and gender parity within marriage. Analyzing attitudes toward topics such as decision-making, women's involvement in stereotypically male roles, and maternal employment across five large-scale studies, Arland Thornton and Linda Young-DeMarco located "dramatic shifts in attitudes and beliefs concerning equality between women and men from the 1960s through the mid-1990s" (2001, 1014). An analysis of changes in American marriage between 1980 and 2000 conducted by Paul Amato and his coauthors has yielded similar results: responses reflected growing individualism and personal choice within marriages (2007, 205), and the percentage of couples who said that they generally shared decision-making equally rose from 49 percent to 64 percent (207).

Additionally, married women's participation in the labor force has continued to rise. In 1970, 41 percent of married women in the United States were engaged in paid work. That figure had grown to 50 percent by 1980, and by 2010 it had climbed to 61 percent (United States Census Bureau 2012). At the same time, women are now outpacing men in terms of educational attainment. In 2009–10, for instance, women earned the majority of college degrees at all levels—associate's, bachelor's, master's, and doctor's (National Center for Education Statistics 2012). Between 1994 and 2012, the share of young women who were enrolled in college immediately out of high school increased from 63 percent to 71 percent, while for men this figure remained constant at 61 percent (Lopez and Gonzalez-Barrera 2014).

Alongside these changes in gender roles, we have seen tighter, more competitive professional job markets, with more workers experiencing greater employment instability, as the job security enjoyed by many in the years after World War II continues to erode and the United States economy increasingly relies upon contingent, shorter-term positions in the place of long-term, stable employment (Stone and Arthurs 2013). In higher education, for example, there has been a slow drying up of the tenure system and an increase in the proportion of non-tenure-track instructors with minimal job security or longevity (American Association of University Professors 2016).[2]

In summary, what we have seen is this: wives, increasingly holding undergraduate and advanced degrees, are working outside the home in larger numbers, and they retain greater decision-making power within their marriages. Additionally, some workers are finding job security harder to attain, and the professional workforce is growing increasingly specialized. Workers move from job to job more frequently, and stable employment geographically close to one's partner becomes less of a possibility. At the same time, both husbands and wives are thinking more individualistically about their aspirations, occupational and otherwise. Throw these historical elements into the blender, and it is the perfect recipe for the commuter marriage.

"I Will Follow Him" . . . or Maybe I Won't: A Literature Gap

Despite the visibility of commuter spouses in the media and the potential importance of this population for understanding broader social patterns, a larger body of work has focused on the opposite phenomenon: dual-career couples who reconcile their geographic conflicts by continuing to live together. Previous scholarship, for instance, has discussed the concept of the "trailing spouse" who "chooses to forsake his or her (typically, her) job to accommodate the other spouse's job relocation" (Shahnasarian 1991, 179), and researchers have explored various dimensions of the decision to trail or not to trail (e.g., Harvey 1995; Linehan and Walsh 2001; McNulty

2012). In a 1992 article, "I Will Follow Him: Family Ties, Gender-Role Beliefs, and Reluctance to Relocate for a Better Job," William Bielby and Denise Bielby discussed wives', but not husbands', reticence to capitalize on job opportunities for themselves in new locations. Since that time, a wealth of research has explored the causes and consequences of the decision to trail or not to trail, particularly among expatriates (e.g., Harvey 1995; Harvey 1998; Harvey and Wiese 1998; Linehan and Walsh 2001; McNulty 2012). In contrast, research on commuter spouses has been sparser.

However, a large body of scholarship has treaded around the edges of this topic. For instance, a number of previous scholarly articles and books have discussed other types of noncohabiting couples. Some research on LAT (living apart together) relationships has examined unmarried couples (Guldner 2003; Haskey and Lewis 2006; Milan and Peters 2003; Stafford and Reske 1990) or has treated married and unmarried noncohabiting couples as one category (Binstock and Thornton 2004; Duncan et al. 2013; M. Holmes 2014; Levin 2004; Levin and Trost 1999; Roseneil 2006). Other scholarship has included commuter spouses as members within a broader category of nontraditional relationships. In Ulrich Beck and Elisabeth Beck-Gernsheim's *Distant Love* (2014), for instance, the authors explore the phenomenon of "world families"—a term encapsulating a variety of types of relationships, ranging from long-distance couples to mixed-nationality couples. Other researchers have looked at spouses who do not live together for a variety of reasons unrelated to marital discord, not simply due to their work (Rindfuss and Stephen 1990), or couples who live apart due to the occupational demands of one spouse but who are not necessarily dual-earners (Zvonkovic et al. 2005).[3] While commuter spouses have been the subject of some relatively recent research (e.g., Bergen 2010a, Bergen 2010b, Bergen 2014, Bergen, Kirby, and McBride 2007, McBride and Bergen 2014; Rhodes 2002), much of which has been written by communications scholars, commuters have not received the same level of scholarly attention as trailing spouses in recent years. Indeed, much scholarship focusing on these couples is based on research from the 1970s and 1980s (Anderson and Spruill 1993; Bunker et al. 1992; Gerstel 1977, 1978; Gerstel and Gross 1982, 1984; Govaerts and Dixon 1988; Gross 1980a, 1980b; Winfield 1985).

This book diverges from these previous studies in several key ways. First, by limiting my focus to spouses (rather than all long-distance couples), I engage directly with a broader literature on changes to the institution of marriage. Locating commuter spouses within this scholarship, I discuss how they both highlight and disrupt some of the large-scale developments in the meaning and shape of this institution. Similarly, by focusing on spouses who live apart due to professional demands (rather than for other reasons), I am able to locate the analysis within a large and timely literature on specialization, the changing characteristics of professional work, and the integration of work and family life.

Yet my analysis also diverges from the older studies that have only focused on spouses. For instance, as discussed in chapter 2, the present study sheds light on how the availability of advanced communication technology changes the game for these couples in some ways (while also creating new wrinkles in their relationships!). To some extent, the present study also reflects changes in gender dynamics that have been occurring since the 1970s and 1980s, when much of the research on this topic was completed. Yet perhaps even more illuminating are my findings that dovetail with this older work. For instance, as I explore in chapters 4 and 5, some of my findings related to gender also bear striking similarities to Gerstel and Gross's research published in 1984. My analysis illustrates the "stickiness" (i.e., persistence) of normative attitudes surrounding gender, family, and work over time.

Research focusing on commuter spouses (Magnuson and Norem 1999), as well as literature in the popular press surrounding the topic (Bennett 2007; Grose 2011), often concentrates on this lifestyle's effects, generally negative but sometimes positive, on the couple or the individuals within it—for instance, from a family counseling perspective (Glotzer and Federlein 2007; Rhodes 2002). This is true of much of the older research as well (Bunker et al. 1992; Govaerts and Dixon 1988; Groves and Horm-Wingerd 1991). This prior scholarship provides an important launch pad for my analysis, which also to some extent examines the effects of living apart on these couples. However, the primary focus of this text is not, per se, the hazards of noncohabitation. Nor is it the benefits.

Instead, I begin by suggesting that commuter spouses are an illuminating group, not only because of their specific relationship dynamics but also because of what they can teach us about contemporary social life on a broader scale. In the chapters that follow, I argue that spouses who live apart are uniquely instructive for thinking about broader structural and cultural processes such as the "individualization" of American marriage; the connection between gender, work, and home; the role of technology in reinforcing and eroding intimate ties; and the nature of professional identity. In sum, I explore several, interwoven questions and themes, all of which fall under the umbrella question of the book: how do these seemingly nonnormative relationships shed light on broader social patterns? I then return to these themes in the conclusion.

Who are the Commuter Spouses in This Book?

Both historically and in the present day, many types of spouses have lived apart for all sorts of reasons, including the demands of traveling occupations (such as sales work, seasonal labor, and construction work), incarceration, institutionalization, immigration, and marital discord. Living apart is relatively common among military spouses, who describe the lifestyle using their own argot, including terms like "geo-bach" (slang for "geographic bachelor"). Additionally, the assumption that families live together has been problematized by literatures concerning, for instance, step-families and LGBT "chosen kin" (Weston 1997).

When I use the term "commuter spouses" (or "commuters") throughout this book, I am focusing on a particular subset of noncohabiting couples: relatively well-educated spouses who live, or have lived, separately in service to their dual professional careers. This is consistent with the way in which some previous scholarship has used the term.[4] The present study is based exclusively on a sample of people who were married, who lived apart for work-related reasons, and who maintained a separate residence for that purpose.

Why These Couples?

As discussed, couples from various sociodemographic groups enter into noncohabitating relationships for a multitude of reasons, so why concentrate on married professionals who live apart for their careers? I focus on this particular subset of long-distance relationships for several reasons.

First, I only include spouses in this study because a major focus is the evolving cultural construction of marriage. This aspect of the study distinguishes it from other work that has collapsed married and unmarried couples into one category.

Second, I concentrate on relatively highly educated professionals because I wanted to explore the dynamics of spouses who were driven into long-distance marriages by specific mechanisms related to my overarching research question—not, for instance, by financial hardship. My aim was to explore the dynamics of couples who, potentially, were able to make choices about their families and careers in ways that might reflect broader trends toward gender-progressive, individualistic marriage.

However, I conceive of "choice" in a relativistic fashion. As Pamela Stone (2007)—who also uses a relatively privileged sample to make points about broader social dynamics in her work on mothers who "opt out" of the labor force—points out, even the choices of relatively well-educated professionals are shaped by broader social institutions and culture. Here, my intent is not to frame my respondents as people who enjoy completely unconstrained agency. Rather, I suggest that these college-educated professionals ostensibly have a level of control over these arrangements in a way that many other types of noncohabiting spouses—for instance, couples separated due to incarceration or the demands of low-wage seasonal work—do not. As Stephanie Coontz has observed, middle-class professionals have relative freedom to make decisions in the interest of their "long-term betterment"—decisions that may be too risky for lower-income families (2000, 294). Thus, I began from the premise that these commuters plausibly had "choice" over these arrangements in the sense that they lived apart not because of dire financial need. And, in fact, this supposition was borne out, as most respondents indicated that they did not live apart due to financial necessity (although, as I discuss in depth in chapter 3, many respondents still did not view their lifestyle through the lens of choice).

Third, while my sample is not reflective of all types of couples who live apart for all reasons, it likely represents one modal category of long-distance marriages. Drawing on data from the 2000 United States Census, Marta Murray-Close has found an elevated prevalence of marital noncohabitation among workers with higher levels of education. For instance, among married (but not "separated") workers in her sample whose highest level of educational attainment was a college degree, 1.9 percent of men and 1.7 percent of women were living apart from their spouses. However, among married workers whose highest degree was a doctorate, 2.9 percent of men and 3.5 percent of women were not cohabitating (2013, 7).[5]

While Murray-Close did not specifically examine spouses who lived apart due to work—as this group is not statistically isolable with any demographic instruments that currently exist (Rindfuss and Stephen 1990, 261)—she made a compelling argument that these findings were related to the highly specialized nature of professional labor markets. The structure of those markets, and the meaning of professional work, are key themes in this book as well.[6]

In sum, I explore several broad, interlocking social dynamics, including the changing shape of the institution of marriage and its relationship to individualization, changing gender roles related to family and career, and the shifting meaning of professional work. Dual-income married professionals who live apart in service to their careers are uniquely positioned to shed light on these particular dynamics.

At the same time, in some respects these married professionals are similar to other types of noncohabitating couples, as well as other types of "atypical" families, and I explore these similarities throughout the book as well. I draw parallels with military spouses; "fly-in, fly-out" (FIFO) husbands who work in the oil, gas, and mining industries; migrant workers and transnational families; divorced co-parents; and couples who maintain separate residences for a variety of reasons beyond career concerns—to give just a few examples. While commuter spouses represent a discrete, relatively homogenous group whose arrangements are forged by specific career-related mechanisms, this analysis contributes to a broader literature on long-distance intimacy more generally.

Homogeneity of the Sample

While much of the uniformity in this sample is by design, it is important to call attention to other potentially problematic similarities among these respondents. For instance, I did not interview any same-sex couples for this book. This was not by design. The initial call for participants specifically mentioned an interest in interviewing same-sex spouses, and I worked through my own networks attempting to recruit same-sex couples for the project. However, as discussed, only married couples were included in the sample because one major focus of the overarching project was the changing meaning and shape of American marriages. Same-sex couples have only recently been afforded universal access to legal marriage in the United States. In the future, extending the project to include noncohabitating same-sex spouses would be, in my opinion, worthwhile and potentially illuminating.

I also specifically worked through my networks to recruit participants of color, though my final sample was predominantly (92.8%) white. My inability to locate many nonwhite participants may be related to the fact that white people are overrepresented in higher education and professional careers. White people are undoubtedly more likely than those of other races to have access to the types of choices I analyze in this study. As I discuss further in appendix A, I also may have oversampled individuals working in academic jobs. It is important to note that these limitations precluded some types of intersectional analysis. However, I do explore other forms of difference, when possible, throughout this book. For example, I look at variations by gender, job type, and parental status.

Organization of the Book

Each chapter contributes to the overarching project of this book by locating commuter spouses within a specific theoretical dialogue relating to a particular area of social life that this group more broadly illuminates and also potentially disrupts. By tapping into, and extending, these broader scholarly conversations, my aim is to explore not only the dynamics of these couples' nonnormative relationships, but also, within every chapter, a particular way in which commuter marriage casts light on a larger-scale social transformation or dynamic.

In chapter 1, I focus on commuter spouses as an outcome and expression of shifts in the meaning of marriage. Previous literature has highlighted the transition toward the individualized marriage, which features an expansion of self-development and a focus on personal choice. I view commuter spouses through the lens of this scholarship, in combination with a broad body of theoretical work—including Anthony Giddens's scholarship on the "pure relationship" (1992, 58)—suggesting that post-modern couples are moving toward more individualistic relationships. I find that, on one hand, commuter couples are an extreme representation of the shift toward individualization, as they are physically separated and they are not engaging in task-sharing on a daily basis. On the other hand, by continually emphasizing the importance of interreliance in their relationships, commuter spouses also demonstrate the durability of collectivist notions about marriage. I conclude the chapter by discussing the broader importance of these findings, which serve as a reminder that the meanings of marriage and the family may be in flux, but we have not abandoned past paradigms, even among those of us who are seemingly exemplars of self-reliance.

Continuing on the theme of interdependence and drawing on prior empirical literature in the communications field and theoretical work on space, chapter 2 explores how commuter spouses navigate their marriages from a distance. I found that commuters often privileged social space and mental space over physical space. For instance, many characterized the houses they shared with their partners as "home," regardless of how much time they personally spent living there. A major factor in their downplaying of physical distance was their ability to remain in continuous contact with their partners via various communication technologies. Drawing on a longstanding communications literature about the impersonal, personal, and "hyperpersonal" (Walther 1996) dimensions of new technologies, I discuss how commuters were able to use different modes of communication for relaying different types of information. Yet these technologies as a whole were not sufficient to fully bridge the gap created by physical separation—a finding that was most apparent in my respondents' discussions about health concerns and child-rearing issues. I conclude the chapter by arguing that, since they live out substantial portions of their relationships through technology, commuter spouses represent a strategic research site at which to analyze the capacity of communication technologies to sustain intimate relationships more generally.

Chapter 3 explores how these couples shed light on the structure and meaning of professional work as well as the concept of "deviance." While few respondents said that financial necessity was the cause of their noncohabitation, nearly half (47.4%) indicated that they lived apart not by choice. The commuters I interviewed were predominantly white, well-educated, relatively high earners in heterosexual marriages. They were people whom we would expect to have access to choices in life, but the way they spoke about their families and their jobs often suggested a dearth of options. I suggest that commuter spouses' perceptions of strain are the result of a concatenation of factors, including highly specialized professional labor markets, a capitalist system that influences individual conceptions of choice, and strong occupational investment. In particular, this chapter reveals the concept of "professional necessity"—a nonagentic, not explicitly financial lens through which these workers view their occupational moves. I conclude the chapter by detailing the importance of these findings, not only for our knowledge of commuter spouses, but also for our understanding of professional identity and the disjuncture between the structure of professional work and family life more generally.

In chapter 4, I discuss commuter spouses within the context of research about gender and the separation of work and domestic spheres. Drawing upon theoretical literature about "doing" and "undoing" gender (e.g., Berk 1985; Risman 2009; West and Zimmerman 1987), I explore how these arrangements enable spouses to engage in atypical gender performances. For instance, noncohabitation benefits women in that it provides the ability to temporarily detach from domestic obligations in order to further one's career. In other ways, however, standard gender roles—particularly surrounding childcare—are crystallized within these relationships. I conclude the chapter by discussing its implications for broader literature on gender, family, and work—a topic that extends into the next chapter.

Chapter 5 follows the thread of gender dynamics in these relationships. However, it moves beyond the topic of work/life integration, contextualizing commuter spouses more generally within literature about the relative advantages and disadvantages of marriage for both men and women. I investigate how the unique benefits and drawbacks of the commuting lifestyle destabilize, but also reflect, cultural norms relating to gender. Commuter spouses provide a novel analytical lens for this topic because they move back and forth between the worlds of solo living and togetherness, and thus are uniquely reflective about what they gain and lose from proximity and from independence. In this way, chapter 5 brings us full circle back to the primary topic of chapter 1: how couples navigate the disjuncture between the norm of spousal interdependence and the move toward individualization.

Chapter 6 begins with a reflection on the question I get asked most often about commuter couples: "Are they happy?" There is no monolithic answer to this question. Some people I interviewed were more content than others. There were elements of these relationships that respondents found positive, or exciting, or uniquely freeing. But, in some ways these relationships replicated broader inequalities—for instance, related to gender. One thing that most of these couples had in common was that they ultimately planned to live together again one day. I unravel why that is, arguing that the elements of their relationships that make these individuals contented or discontented are important for understanding not only these couples' dynamics but also broader structural and cultural changes in marriage, gender, family, and professional work in the United States.

Finally, in the conclusion, I retrace the central themes of the text. I discuss how they intersect with prior theoretical and empirical research, and I ruminate further on their relevance for future research, policy, and broader discussions about gender, work, and the family in the twenty-first century.

A Note on Autoethnography

Throughout these chapters, I include elements of autoethnography: Carolyn Ellis's (2004) term for dealing with the experiences and emotions of the researcher as subject matter in and of themselves. While this book is not "an autoethnography" per se, I follow in the footsteps of previous researchers who have dealt autoethnographically with research on distance relationships (M. Holmes 2010) by infusing brief self-narratives throughout this book. I do this for two reasons.

First, these narratives are an additional source of detailed, "thick" (Geertz 1994) information about a noncohabitating spouse. To exclude them would be to ignore available data, and their inclusion lends texture to the book. Second, I engage in this "self-inscription" (Reed-Danahay 2001, 407) in order to be very transparent about my own positionality from the first sentence of this book. I include "the 'I,'" as Ellis puts it (2004, xix), into my work so that I might be as upfront as possible, both to readers and to myself, about my "insider" position as someone going through a circumstance similar to those of my respondents. Through this subjectivity, I have also found greater objectivity, in the sense that repeatedly acknowledging my subject position also has allowed me to interrogate, and hopefully transcend, my own biases.

As the stories throughout this book suggest, the people I interviewed had a diversity of experiences. I find that many of the overall findings resonate with my personal story, but some do not—a reaction that would likely be shared by any of my respondents who may read this book. I have strived to look at personal experiences in order to understand a broader social phenomenon and to see the links between the two—a major goal of both autoethnography and social science more broadly (Mills 2000).

Goals for the Book

It is my wish that scholars will find this book important not only for what it can tell us about these particular couples—their unique struggles and triumphs and how they negotiate meaning and identity in their atypical relationships. I hope that readers will also find it compelling because commuter spouses, despite living in nonnormative arrangements, are extreme embodiments of many of the evolutions that have been taking place in American life, both at work and in the home, over the past half a century. At the same time, these couples illuminate the durability of cultural conceptions about gender and the family, even within their nontraditional and seemingly highly individualistic arrangements.

Additionally, while I focus explicitly on these relationships within an American context, it is my hope and intent that these stories will have resonance outside of the United States as well. In fact, recent research focusing on various types of noncohabitating couples has largely been conducted outside of the United States (e.g., Beck and Beck-Gernsheim 2014; Duncan et al. 2013; M. Holmes 2014). The fact that there have been many non-U.S. studies of long-distance couples suggests that the large-scale changes that have created commuter marriages also resonate on a global level. Indeed, I draw on this cross-national scholarship throughout the book.

Along similar lines, at the same time that commuter spouses are an extreme iteration of broad social transformations, many of my observations and conclusions may also apply to unmarried commuter couples and others living in atypical arrangements. I draw parallels with these groups throughout the book as well.

The meaning of marriage in the United States is, and will continue to be, in contention, and public policies regarding the regulation of family status will continue to be in dispute and to shift. Noncohabitating spouses encapsulate not only many facets of the changing American family but also changes in social structure and meaning outside of the family as well. On one hand, these couples are extreme manifestations of large-scale historical shifts: toward individualism in intimate relationships, toward contingent but highly specialized labor, and toward greater gender parity in the home and at work. But on the other hand, these couples tell a compelling story about the stickiness of historical ideals relating to gender, marriage, the family, and work. Ultimately, this book is not merely about professionals who live apart from their husbands or wives due to occupational demands. Rather, it suggests that there are broader lessons to be learned from the way they live their lives.

1

APART TOGETHER

Individualism, Interdependence, and the Meaning of (Commuter) Marriage

Virginia and Bob

Virginia was talking about marriage. Describing herself as "not the girl with, like, the Barbie dolls and playing wedding and planning my wedding," she emphasized that for much of her life, she had not envisioned herself tying the knot. When I spoke with her in the summer of 2012, she had been married for four years and had been living apart from her husband for the last three. Separated by a two-hour drive in different regions of the same state, the couple generally reunited every weekend. They did not think of either of their residences as shared, and they had no children.

A small-business owner in her late thirties, Virginia was the first person I interviewed for this project. Although I did not plan it this way, perhaps it is fitting, then, that she finds her way into chapter 1. Easygoing and extremely forthcoming, she spoke to me like a pal from college who was playing catch-up. When I asked about her reasons for marrying Bob, she reflected that she had wanted their relationship to be "solid" and "substantial." "It's nice—knowing there's somebody in the universe who is kind of like your partner," she told me. "You know, people say that all the time, 'I like having a partner.' But to me that sounds like a business partner or something. You know, to me it's more than that. It's like somebody who's your soul partner. And being apart doesn't diminish it. Being apart diminishes our communication, it diminishes our sex life, it diminishes all this stuff. But that connection that you have—like, time and space, it doesn't matter." Yet, despite her emphasis on the partnership aspect of marriage, Virginia also characterized herself as "independent" and driven in her career.

Several weeks later, I interviewed her husband Bob, age fifty-nine, who worked in the construction industry, and I asked him the same question about his reasons for getting married. Bob responded, "I didn't want to just date. After two years, I wanted to marry her and I wanted her to get the benefits that I had to offer. And I wanted the benefits that she had to offer me." When I inquired about these "benefits," he spoke about financial stability and emotional support. However, when I asked how he and Virginia relied on each other, Bob characterized that as a "hard question," proclaiming, "We're both pretty independent!" He then launched into the friendly laughter that often punctuated our interview.

Viewing themselves as "independent" individuals pursuing personal fulfillment, as well as "soul partners" who functioned as a unit, Virginia and Bob are protagonists in two major stories about marriage in the contemporary United States. These stories may seem paradoxical, but they are not mutually exclusive. On one hand, there is the story about how marriages are increasingly choice centered, individualistic, and egalitarian. On the other hand, there is also a story about durable cultural ideals and married couples who continue to feel incredibly interdependent and enmeshed.

In this chapter, I argue that commuter spouses—couples who choose to get and remain married yet are ostensibly so invested in their individual career goals that they do not cohabitate—are instructive as extreme examples of this broader cultural disjuncture within American life. My respondents engaged in two discourses about marriage that operated in tension. Although they positioned themselves as highly autonomous, interdependence was a key theme in their responses as well. Specifically, it came out in a discourse about "apart togetherness." Perhaps more surprising, a substantial minority of respondents described how the practical demands of their living-apart arrangements, in combination with contemporary communication technologies (discussed in more depth in the next chapter), actually facilitated their interconnectedness. By continually emphasizing the importance of interreliance in their relationships, my respondents demonstrate the stickiness of some ideals and practices relating to marriage.

Putting the "I" in Marriage: The Historical Shift toward Individualization

One narrative about the changing American family highlights its increased emphasis on spousal independence and personal fulfillment. Beginning in the latter part of the twentieth century, according to scholars who make this claim, marriage—in the United States and elsewhere—became increasingly "individualized" (Amato et al. 2007; Cancian 1990; Cherlin 2004; Cherlin 2009; Coontz 2005). People began entering into the institution increasingly for the emotional support, intimacy, and romantic love it provided, and they increasingly felt free to exit their relationships when they were no longer receiving these benefits (Cherlin 2009; Giddens 1992). Within this paradigm, the two partners were increasingly independent and less likely than spouses in the past to focus on conforming to socially defined roles, such as the "good parent" or "supportive spouse" (Cherlin 2004, 853). This transition was related to the decline of the male breadwinner–female homemaker model, decreasing task specialization between the genders, the increasing democratization of marital decision-making, and the increasing ability of each partner to provide financially for himself or herself. In short, within individualized marriage, as the moniker suggests, spouses became two distinct individuals pursuing autonomous goals.

Scholars suggest that this shift occurred when it did for a few reasons. Sociologist Andrew Cherlin (2009), for example, points out that basic material needs were less of a concern for the generation who grew up during the prosperity of the 1950s than they had been for previous generations; subsequently, this cohort of adults could turn toward higher-order goals. These goals manifested in, among other things, the rise in alternatives to marriage, such as premarital sex and cohabitation. In the present day, reliance on a spouse has become less of a concern and "personal choice and self-development loom large in people's construction of their marital careers" (Cherlin 2004, 853).[1]

"All You Need Is Love"?: Commuter Spouses and the "Pure Relationship"

In sum, according to the individualization thesis, postmodern marriages (and relationships in general) have shifted away from interdependence toward individualization and a simultaneous emphasis on both love and autonomy. The thesis, moreover, ties into a broader literature depicting a contemporary landscape in which the ties that bind partners are fragile and largely symbolic (Bauman 2003; Beck and Beck-Gernsheim 1995; Beck-Gernsheim 2002; Sennett 1998).

Perhaps the most salient theoretical exploration of this shift toward individualization has appeared in the work of sociologist Anthony Giddens (1992). In particular, Giddens used the term "pure relationship" to refer to a form of intimate bond "where a social relation is entered into for its own sake, for what can be derived by each person from a sustained association with another; and which is continued only in so far as it is thought by both parties to deliver enough satisfactions for each individual to stay within it" (58). Giddens's formulation has not gone without critique. Sociologist Mary Holmes (2004a, 2004b), for instance, suggests that Giddens fails to adequately address men's and women's unequal ability to be autonomous, when women have a greater burden as caretakers (a theme I discuss in detail in chapter 4) and experience stronger pressure to make compromises. (See also Jamieson 1999.) Further, it is important to note that Giddens does not view the pure relationship as tied to marriage or any other social institution. Still, Giddens's notion that society is moving toward a "posttraditional" model is part of a broader argument about how couples are now viewing relationships as a means toward self-development. The concept of a pure relationship is thus a useful analytical tool for thinking about the important historical and cultural position occupied by commuter spouses.[2]

When Virginia talked to me about marriage, she was looking at the institution through a very specific sociohistoric lens. Her description of Bob as her "soul partner," more than her "business partner," makes sense within a particular paradigm where spouses value affective attachment in addition to (and, by some accounts, over) tangible material benefits. Similarly, in his discussion of the benefits of marriage, Bob articulated almost to the word Giddens's notion of the relationship that exists "for what can be derived by each person from a sustained association with another" (1992, 58).

It is not a leap to think of commuter spouses as an extreme manifestation of this emphasis on self-fulfillment. Indeed, in their 1984 book on commuter spouses, Gerstel and Gross explicitly made this claim: "Commuter marriage is a structure spawned by this ideology of individualism which emphasizes that each spouse's worth depends on individual achievements rather than on family membership" (13). In fact, I would take their argument a step further. Not only was the cultural shift toward self-reliance a major catalyst for the commuter marriage, but the commuter marriage then also becomes a strategic location at which to observe this shift. Spouses who live apart for their careers become potentially key players in this overall drama of individualization, as their noncohabitating relationships serve as kind of a laboratory in which we can investigate these social changes in an amplified form.

Putting the "We" in "Wedding": Marital Interdependence

Then there is the second story, which suggests that—despite a broadening cultural emphasis on personal autonomy—the institution of marriage today remains a dominant force in shaping American social organization. Although Americans are now entering into marriage at later ages (Wang and Parker 2014), and marriage rates differ based on factors such as race (Cherlin 1992; Schoen and Kluegel 1988; Wilson 1987) and socioeconomic status (Edin and Kefalas 2011; Gibson-Davis, Edin, and McLanahan 2005; Edin and Reed 2005; Smock, Manning, and Porter 2005), a majority of adults in the United States still get married (Wang and Parker 2014). Additionally, despite the rise in alternatives to marriage, such as premarital sex and cohabitation (Cherlin 2009), the symbolic significance of marriage "has remained high and may even have increased" (Cherlin 2004, 848). Indeed, the persistent cultural importance of marriage can be seen in the institution's pivotal role in the gay rights movement (Stacey 2012, 3). As sociologist Kathleen Gerson (2009) has explained, "The ideal of permanent marriage persists for relationships despite the fluid and uncertain nature of intimate commitment" (736). In sum, despite challenges to the institution, a large number of Americans continue to embrace the cultural ethos of marriage (Hill and Yeung 1999; Thornton and Young-Demarco 2001).

These dual commitments to both personal autonomy and the institution of marriage create a cultural tension that has not gone unnoticed by scholars (Bellah et al. 2007). As Cherlin (2009) has summarized, "The United States is unique among nations in its strong support for marriage, on one hand, and its postmodern penchant for self-expression and personal growth, on the other hand" (2). These two seemingly paradoxical orientations toward relationships have uneasily fused to become part of the bedrock of American social life.

Defining "Individualism" and "Interdependence" for Commuter Spouses

Throughout this chapter, I use the terms "individualism" and "autonomy" interchangeably to describe instances in which spouses characterized themselves as independent or interpreted marriage as facilitative of their individual goals—for instance, as a path to personal happiness, self-fulfillment, or self-development. In contrast, I use "interdependence" and "interconnectedness" interchangeably to connote instrumental reliance—for instance, task sharing. Interestingly, although a body of theoretical work has focused on the tension between these two cultural goals, few researchers have examined how couples themselves view these dynamics as operating within their marriages—that is, how these seemingly conflicting ideals play out "on the ground." Commuter spouses who choose to get married and remain married yet live apart to pursue individual careers become instructive as extreme examples of this broader cultural disjuncture.

Individualism and Interdependence in the Commuter Marriage

Most respondents, like Virginia and Bob, talked about both individualism and interconnection. Although I did not ask respondents specifically about their feelings of autonomy in their marriages, many spontaneously emphasized this aspect of their relationships. When asked if they had any advice for other potential commuters, for example, many emphasized that the relationship style "worked" for them because they were already highly autonomous. For instance, Jeff maintained, "[My wife] doesn't *need* me to live a healthy life. She's very self-assured, as am I. . . . And she's independent. She doesn't *need* me to be there. So I think that's important, on both sides" (emphasis in original).

In addition, when asked "What would you say you like the most about being married?," many commuters emphasized their partners' contributions to their own personal growth. For example, Simon, a twenty-six-year-old government employee, replied, "She's been so great at being both a guide and encouraging me to guide as well. And I think it's been very helpful for me to have such open communication and have somebody who's willing to give me helpful criticisms to develop into a better person."

Jeff and Simon both emphasized autonomy and the importance of marriage as a vehicle for self-development—framings that resonate strongly with Cherlin's (2004) notion of the individualized marriage in which "personal choice and self-development loom large" (853) and Giddens's (1992) broader conception of a relationship driven by what each partner can personally gain from it.

Based on this evidence, it might be tempting to think of commuters only as people who embody autonomous, symbolic marriage and to close the book on them. However, that would only tell part of the story. Yes, commuter marriages tend to be highly individualized. However, when we zoom in on these relationships and analyze the nuance, we begin to see that commuter spouses do think of themselves as dependent upon their partners, despite their geographic separation.

Interconnectedness emerged as a particularly salient theme in responses to the question "In what ways would you say that you and [your spouse] rely on each other?"[3] Although it may be unsurprising that this question would prompt discussions about interdependence, it is revealing that no respondents replied "not at all." Moreover, the ways these respondents said they were reliant on their partners were telling. More than one-quarter (27.3%) of respondents indicated that they relied on their partners for help with household tasks, despite the fact that, in most cases, they were not living together in the same household the majority of the time. The same number of interviewees mentioned financial reliance, and about one-quarter discussed cooperative child-rearing (25.0%). Further, it is important to point out that only one respondent mentioned exclusively emotional reliance on her partner and no other forms of reliance. But perhaps the most salient finding from these responses was that over one-fifth of commuters (23.9%) indicated that they relied on their partners in every way. Jeff, for instance, whom I quoted above emphasizing the independence of both partners in his marriage, had a seemingly paradoxical reply to this question: "I would say we're sort of relying on each other for everything."

Art and Gretchen

Art (a government employee in his late thirties) and Gretchen (an engineer in her late forties) had been married for about a year. The couple had never cohabitated. Art—who took a plane ride to see Gretchen and her teenaged daughter (from a previous relationship) every three to four weeks—emphasized his continual reliance on his wife, despite their physical separation. He referred to their kind of interconnectedness as "tech support":

> *In what ways would you say that you and your wife rely on each other?*
> Art: Hmm. I don't know, I'd say mainly just for support in whatever it is that we're doing.
> *You mean like emotional support, or other forms of support?*
> Art: No, more like "tech support"—I guess I don't know how to say it. So she'll be in the middle of something and she needs something—she'll just either call me or text me to ask me to do something, or look something up. Or vice versa. I'll be lost on a bike ride and call her [*laughs*].

Gretchen, too, underscored the constant nature of their communication, observing, "I think for both of us when anything happens, we just want to immediately talk to each other." Art and Gretchen's responses to this question and Art's notion of "tech support" were indicative of how many respondents discussed their relationships. Like Art, many commuters underscored how integrated their partners were in their everyday activities despite their geographic separation.

However, this framing coexisted alongside a parallel narrative about spousal autonomy. Art, for instance, also repeatedly emphasized that he and his wife were independent individuals who led their own lives; for that reason, he indicated, "[Living apart is] an inconvenience but it doesn't really affect our relationship, I don't think." While in some ways these couples embodied the individualization thesis, in other ways interdependence also "loomed large" (to borrow Cherlin's words) in their marriages.

"Just Because You Don't See Each Other, It Doesn't Mean You're Not Together"

The responses of these couples to the question asking about reliance suggested that, for the most part, they did think of themselves as units—as connected despite their physical separation. In fact, a common theme that emerged in interviews was the concept of "apart togetherness."[4] Nearly one-half of all respondents (n=47, 48.5%) engaged with this theme at some point during their interviews. For instance, when I asked, "What do you like the most about being married?," Katie, a banking professional in her mid-thirties, replied that she enjoyed having her husband "there," adding "We've learned that just because you don't see each other, it doesn't mean you're not together." As Dorinda put it, "You know, there's always someone around, even when he's not physically around." These were typical responses to this question. Eighty respondents received this question and, perhaps paradoxically for noncohabitating couples, "enjoying each other's company" (n=33; 41.3%) and "companionship" (n=24; 30.0%) emerged as the most prevalent themes.

Respondents who spoke about companionship did not solely focus on being or feeling connected on an abstract level; rather, they discussed task sharing and cooperation between partners. For example, Matthew, the sixty-year-old director of a nonprofit, had been living a four-hour drive away from his wife Trudy for about twelve years. They saw each other on the weekends. When asked what he liked most about being married,

Matthew was one of the respondents who replied "companionship," adding, "It's strange I say that, right?" Further, when asked how he and Trudy relied on each other, Matthew replied, "There's clearly an emotional reliance. There's a kind of practical reliance on just the business of running a family and a household and all of that. Emotional and practical." Matthew's description of collectively "running a household" is an example of how respondents used the rhetoric of interdependence to frame their relationships. Matthew emphasized both the emotional and task-sharing aspects of marriage, despite the fact that he and his wife had not lived in the same household, except on weekends, for over a decade.

The fact that so many respondents drew on the theme of togetherness is particularly compelling in light of the amount of time these couples spent apart. To put this finding in perspective, about one-third of my interviewees (33.0%, n=32) typically saw their partners less than every two weeks, whereas 13.4 percent (n=13) reunited about every two weeks, and 53.6 percent (n=52) saw their spouses at least once a week (typically over the weekends). Most of the couples in this sample were spending more time living apart than together, and in many cases substantially more time apart. Yet, in their own words, they were apart "together"—functioning as part of a dyad, despite their ostensibly individualistic relationships. Their concept of "apart togetherness" is perhaps a fitting descriptor for the broader cultural directive that we pursue self-fulfillment, but that we do it while legally and emotionally bound to another person.

Distance Brings Us Closer?

Perhaps one of my most surprising findings was that a substantial minority of interviewees felt that living apart actually facilitated their interdependence. Not only did many respondents emphasize the frequency of their contact while apart, but some also suggested that the distance in fact improved their connections with their spouses.[5] For example, one female commuter made this point, explaining, "Because when we're home we're so consumed with the day-to-day stuff that sometimes we forget to just stop and just talk. But when he's gone, every evening we both kind of sit down and we have a pretty lengthy conversation." Another respondent, who had recently resumed living with her husband, told me, similarly, "One thing that I hate, though, is that now I don't ever hear from him during the day. He just doesn't call. . . . We talk less during the day [than we did when we lived apart]. And I hate that. I wish he'd learn to respond more, but he really doesn't."

Although many commuter spouses, like Art above, emphasized their ability to perform tasks as a unit while apart via various communication technologies, some went even further. They indicated that living apart necessitated—and, thus, entailed—a higher level of communication than cohabitation did. Although I did not ask respondents if living apart had improved their relationships, this theme emerged in response to the open-ended question asking whether there was anything they liked about living apart, and if so, what. The most common response was that they felt they could be more productive or get more work done (75.3%). However, a substantial minority of respondents (25.8%) replied that noncohabitation had improved their marriages in some ways. Some indicated that their separation had drawn the couple "closer" or given the relationship "spice," whereas others described the short periods of time they now spent together as a return to the excitement of dating.[6] For example, one commuter told me that a "weird benefit" of noncohabitation was that it brought "something fresh" to her relationship. "What I've found in these few short months is that we're actually communicating a lot more overall than we were, I think, than when we were living together," she explained. "One of the texts I got today was just a little joke. And that hasn't happened in a long time. So I think it is something about the distance—it almost brings you back to when you are first meeting someone and you don't live together and you don't see them. And so you are kind of flirting a little bit and introducing yourself." These types of responses suggested that one positive aspect of living apart, for some commuter spouses, was that it surprisingly facilitated togetherness—a concept that worked on both instrumental and emotional levels.

Let's Talk about Sex: "Apart Togetherness" and Physical Intimacy

Virginia was talking about sex. After I had asked all of my questions, we continued chatting, and she mentioned that she was surprised that I "didn't have more of those types of questions in there." (As discussed further in appendix A, I saved questions about potentially sensitive topics such as sex for the follow-up survey.) Virginia went on to say that this area had caused tension in her relationship with Bob:

> I'll actually go ahead and tell you about this: we do have arguments about sex. And it's because, like when he comes on the weekend it's just like, he's a man. He can do it any time, any place. And I just said, "It's really hard being like clockwork" [*snaps fingers*], and sometimes you're just tired. Or you're not in the mood. So, it's like the communication thing where we kind of like, go back and forth between—because it is one of those things, you drive a long time, and you're tired but you only have two days. Two days. And then you feel this pressure. So we do have arguments about that. Because he's always like, "We don't do it enough," and I'm like, "We're fine. We live apart. We have all these other things." So we argue about that.

Interestingly, while one might guess that commuters have less sex than the average married couple (if simply because of time constraints), previous research findings have been mixed in that respect. Gerstel and Gross (1984), for instance, found that the impact of the commuting relationship on frequency of sexual activity varied, ranging from nearly no impact to a substantial one (62). Additionally, like Virginia, some of the commuters in their sample reported feeling pressure to engage in sex during the periods they were together (64). My follow-up survey, which asked respondents to write in how often they typically had sex while living the commuter lifestyle, revealed an average of 5.8 times per month.[7] By comparison, the national average for married couples is about seven times a month (Lauman et al. 1994).[8] This disparity suggests that the commuters in my sample may have sex less frequently than noncommuters—though perhaps not dramatically less frequently. Additionally, asked on the follow-up survey "How would you rate your level of satisfaction with your sex life?," only 7.1 percent of my respondents indicated "not at all satisfied," while 19.0 percent said "somewhat satisfied," 45.2 percent said "moderately satisfied," 26.2 percent replied "extremely satisfied," and 2.3 percent said they were "unsure."[9] My findings, like Gerstel and Gross's, suggest that commuters had a diversity of experiences when it came to physical intimacy, but that the lifestyle was not uniformly negative for respondents' sex lives.

One might also expect that the increased freedom built into these arrangements might result in higher rates of adultery. When it came to sexual fidelity, Gerstel and Gross (1984) found that, while nearly one-third of their respondents had affairs while commuting, they were not more likely to have affairs after they started commuting than they did while they were living together—and, in fact, the rates of marital infidelity were similar to those found in the general population (105). Yet other research has suggested that noncohabiting couples have a surprisingly low rate of sexual infidelity; by one estimate, they are about half as likely to be unfaithful as their counterparts who cohabitate (Winfield 1985). Among my respondents, one told me about a flirtation with a colleague, but none talked about being unfaithful—though it is important to note that I did not ask.

Some, however, spontaneously indicated that they had been faithful and that they trusted their partners, despite their geographic separation. For instance, one respondent volunteered: "I'll be very honest, I've never cheated on her. I'm very loyal. Focused on my job and focused on my family." Later in the interview, he added, "I never stayed up nights wondering, 'Gee, I hope my wife isn't fooling around.'" However, he also added that he was aware of infidelity among other commuter spouses in his industry.

While it would be foolish to interpret my respondents' lack of personal stories about infidelity as a lack of infidelity—and it is important to note that I did not interview any former commuter spouses who were now divorced, among whom infidelity may have been more prevalent—my findings, at the very least, do not suggest that commuter marriages are hotbeds of adultery. In fact, like prior scholarship, they demonstrate that commuter marriages are not a monolith when it comes to sexual dynamics. In sum, we might expect commuters' sex lives to reflect the "apartness" of these relationships, with diminished intimacy and higher rates of infidelity. And indeed, some respondents, like Virginia, mentioned that living apart had negatively impacted their sex lives. At the same time, as discussed above, others indicated that noncohabitation had brought the sexual "spice" back into their relationships. Still others seemed neutral about the impact of geographic separation on their sex lives. In a sense, sex was a microcosm for both the "apartness" and "togetherness" of these lifestyles, reflecting how noncohabitation could render these couples either more independent or more enmeshed—or neither.

Outliers

While most commuter spouses spoke about both their autonomy and their interdependence, there were some outliers. Four respondents did not discuss individualism in relation to their marriages. However, I did not ask respondents about their senses of independence or autonomy in their marriages; these respondents may have spoken to these themes if asked directly. In addition, a few respondents made only very minimal references to interdependence. When asked in what ways she relied on her partner, for instance, one respondent told me, "For health insurance. That's about it." These outliers are important to point out because they underscore the fact that interconnectedness and autonomy for these respondents were not 0/1 propositions, but rather gradients. There were both qualitative and quantitative distinctions in the ways different respondents addressed both of these themes.

Still, despite the fact that these spouses were living separately, most framed their relationships both individualistically and in terms of interdependence. Their emphasis on independence was perhaps less surprising—given their noncohabitation, and given prior literature on the shift toward individualized marriage—than the examples of interconnectedness that infused their descriptions of their marriages.

Caveats

While I have characterized commuter spouses as potentially extreme examples of the shift toward personal autonomy, other types of couples might come closer to the archetype of the individualized relationship. Perhaps unmarried couples who live apart would interpret their relationships more individualistically than my respondents—although, of course, unmarried couples would not shed light on the tension between individualism and collectivist notions of marriage. Further, if the cultural valuation of individualism in marriage exists on a spectrum, we might expect the couples most strongly invested in their personal goals to be the ones who can most easily break their ties and select divorce. Because everyone I interviewed for this project was still married, those relationships potentially most individualistic were not represented in this project.[10] However, for these reasons commuter spouses are such an apt population for exploring the cultural tension at the heart of this chapter: they are both highly individualistic and interdependent.

Finally, to find couples who more fully embody the individualization thesis, we might turn to spouses who live apart as a matter of personal preference, because they feel that lifestyle suits them better. Commuter spouses, on the other hand, interpret their noncohabitation as the result of professional exigency—a topic I explore in chapter 3.

The Past Is Always with Us: Conclusions

A wealth of literature emerging in the past few decades has suggested that marriages, and intimate relationships more broadly, are becoming more individualistic and more fragile, and that spouses are continuing to interpret marriage as symbolically important while relying on each other less. At the same time, scholars have pointed to the durability of traditional notions about marriage and the salience of the tension between these cultural emphases on individualism (particularly in the United States) and interdependence. In this chapter, I have argued that commuter spouses reflect this tension in an amplified form.

The fact that my interviewees still viewed themselves as enmeshed with their spouses despite their separateness speaks to the entrenched nature of traditional notions about marriage. Even in this nonnormative form of marriage, commuters interpreted their relationships as not just about love and personal fulfillment. They did, predictably, interpret their relationships within these cultural rubrics, but not only within these rubrics. By and large, they did not discuss their marriages as relationships that existed purely "for [their] own sake" (Giddens 1992).

Of course, one might argue that there is a potential disconnect between what these respondents told me and what they did in practice. Perhaps these commuter spouses overemphasized their interdependence in order to symbolically legitimate their nontraditional marriages. In some ways, their discussions of their marriages played into cultural tropes about marriage and relationships more broadly. Julia Carter (2012), for instance, interviewed women between the ages of nineteen and thirty and discovered that a variety of persistent themes—for instance, fidelity, love, and longevity—emerged for them as important aspects of commitment in romantic relationships. Similarly, for her book *Talk of Love: How Culture Matters* (2013), sociologist Ann Swidler found that middle-class white suburbanites drew from "a common set of cultural motifs" (5) about love (although her main point was that they varied in how they put these motifs into action). Maybe my respondents, like Carter's and Swidler's, were drawing upon familiar cultural themes in order to locate their atypical arrangements within a culturally accepted model. Jan E. Dizard and Howard Gadlin (1992) have noted the irony of the fact that increased autonomy "produces longings for the sorts of solidaristic associations that the family has historically provided, precisely because the decline of such associations greatly intensifies anxieties about identity. The result is a general tendency to romanticize the family even as more and more of us abandon its traditional and solidaristic features" (154). This effect may explain part of what is happening here, with these nontraditional couples interpreting their marriages within a traditional framework. Similarly, commuter spouses' desire to emphasize their connectedness may have something to do with stigma management (Goffman [1963] 2009)—a topic I discuss in greater depth in chapter 3. Asked if they had ever felt judged negatively for their lifestyle, a majority of respondents (n=64; 66.0%) responded in the affirmative. It might make sense for these couples to engage in a form of "accounting" (Goffman 1959; see also Bergen 2010a)—a telling of narratives designed to legitimize their seemingly nonnormative marriages.[11] However, in the present study there was no relationship between discussing "apart togetherness" and responding "yes" to the question about judgment.[12]

Commuter spouses are people who, in some senses, are highly individualistic. But they are also people who seemingly value their marriages and families about as much, if not more so, than cohabitating couples.[13] For example, according to a 2010 Pew research study, about half (51%) of Americans said that they had a closer relationship with their spouse or partner than their parents had with each other; among my respondents, it was 59 percent.[14] And about three-quarters of both my respondents (77%) and Americans (76%) said that family was the most important element in their lives.[15] Further, while it is possible that my respondents were overselling the traditional nature of their arrangements by deploying motifs of connectedness, the very fact of them doing this would suggest the cultural resonance of such notions, even within these atypical relationships.[16]

These motifs are a part of the fundamental cultural tension I outlined at the beginning of this chapter. On one hand, commuter couples are central players in a story about autonomy within marriage and, more broadly, about the increasing fragility of human ties. On the other hand, they suggest that even as we have made these shifts, there is a certain cultural stickiness to more traditional ideas of what marriage entails—a stickiness that persists even among spouses who are seemingly so motivated by their individual career goals that they do not cohabitate.

Indeed, this finding challenges some previous assumptions about these couples. For example, in a *New York Times* article about spouses who live apart (Brooke 2006), Dr. Scott Haltzman, a clinical assistant professor of psychiatry at Brown University, makes the point, "One of the challenges of marriage is to learn how to live with a person and integrate that person into your life. By living apart, you are losing the opportunity to gain that level of intimacy and cooperation." My respondents problematize these notions that commuter couples lack emotional closeness and fail to engage cooperatively in tasks.[17]

Of course, I am certainly not the first one to suggest that, when it comes to marriage, the past is always with us. Other research, too, has pointed to the durability of certain cultural meanings surrounding marriage and the family. One study looking across thirty-one national contexts found, for instance, that despite the trend toward individualization, most spouses continued to pool their money (Lauer and Yodanis 2011). Along similar lines, other work has indicated that people's attitudes about marriage and the family often do not align with any one value set. Swidler found that, when it comes to thoughts about love, "most people do not actually have a single, unified set of attitudes or beliefs" (2013, 4). The importance of both instrumental reliance and cultural meaning can also be seen in contemporary political debates surrounding marriage—for example, in arguments for same-sex marriage that have emphasized the tangible benefits as well as the symbolic importance of the institution itself.

Our interpretations of marriage and the family in the contemporary United States have changed in some ways, but we have not abandoned the past. Commuter spouses reflect this theme more broadly. From an aerial view, they resemble embodiments of the individualized marriage. However, when we focus on their narratives, we see that they talk about their lives as intertwined in multiple practical ways despite their geographic separation. In one sense they reflect the move toward individualization in one of its most extreme manifestations, in another sense, the rigidity of historical notions about marriage in the United States.

And what about beyond the United States? Though I have explored these relationships within an American context, where individualism dominates as a cultural value, it is important to emphasize that the individualization thesis has resonance beyond this country as well. Indeed, Giddens himself is British. Moreover, while in some ways, the United States is uniquely and persistently individualistic (for instance, in its approach to social programs such as healthcare and welfare), non-U.S. scholars have engaged with, and problematized, the individualization thesis in their work on geographically separate couples as well (e.g., M. Holmes 2004a, 2014; Smart and Shipman 2004). Indeed, some of my discussions in this chapter have been relevant to, and contribute to, work on geographically separate families outside of the United States. For example, in her research on transnational families conducted in Australia, Ireland, the Netherlands, Iran, Singapore, and New Zealand, Raelene Wilding (2006) has discussed how communication technologies enable some family members to temporarily overlook their geographic separation and to feel connected. In the next chapter, I further explore how such technologies facilitate interconnectedness for commuter couples.

2

VIRTUALLY TOGETHER

Space, Place, and Communication Technologies

Alexis and Jim

Alexis was talking to me about Facetime. One of her shared rituals with her husband Jim was "going grocery shopping together." Though Alexis and Jim lived fourteen hours apart, the couple would connect virtually via Facetime—she on her iPhone, he on his tablet—as they strode down their respective supermarket aisles, selecting food. Later, at their respective homes, they would cook meals "together."

Pleasant and jokingly self-deprecating in her interview, Alexis—a government employee in her mid-twenties—frequently spoke about her love for Jim and her excitement about their future. Both Alexis and Jim also repeatedly mentioned their church and religious principles as being central to the way they saw the world. When I conducted their interviews, they had been married for about two and a half years and were living apart for the second time. They had no children, though both indicated that this was a plan for the future, when they were reunited.

Alexis told me that while she was away from Jim, she did not go out on the weekends, explaining, "I'm more of a homebody. I'd rather just sit and watch a movie and have him on Facetime. And even though he's not here, just having his little face on the screen—just to know that he's there. And it's not even that we have to talk but just psychologically knowing that someone is there. So he'll watch a movie and he'll hang out with the cat, and every now and then I'll look over and every so often I think that we have a normal relationship when we don't. [*Laughs.*]"[1]

In addition to their Facetiming, Alexis and Jim both discussed other ways that they connected during the time they were apart. Alexis, for instance, emphasized that, the day I interviewed her, she and Jim had talked on the phone three times already. She added that she appreciated the "constant contact" they had, even if it only consisted of him texting "I love you" or the lyrics to a song. Another way the couple stayed in touch was through shared electronic bank statements. "It is kinda nice, just as an affirmation," Alexis explained, "not that I'd ever think he would ever lie to me because I'm pretty sure I know his every move and when he *is* lying—but, yeah, I think it does add a little bit of a comfort or whatever, so I can see what he is doing. And it always is nice to see, like, the checks deposited at church when he's tithing and stuff. In that sense, it gives me affirmation, I guess. Even when I'm not there he's still consistent in the way that he acts" (emphasis in original). Alexis said that these shared statements were "our little link," then laughed as she added, "If we're having long days and we can't talk, at least he can see where I went to lunch or something. I know that sounds kind of twisted."

Jim, also in his mid-twenties, worked as an engineer. He was more laconic than his wife, though he opened up when discussing how the couple remained in touch during their geographic separations. Indeed, like some of the respondents I discussed in the previous chapter, Jim suggested that the distance had improved the couple's communication in some ways. "I actually think it's made us closer over the years," he told me.

Oh, really; how so?
Jim: [I'm] kinda forced—um, well, y'know, I don't know if this is the best word, but I'm kinda forced to talk to her every day. [*laughs*]

Jim: And you have to talk to 'em and, you have to talk—[if] there's a problem, you can't just let it, like, fizzle and just go away. Y'know, you've
gotta talk about it, you've gotta get it out . . . I think it's made us a lot
closer.

Alexis and Jim were atypical interviewees in that they spoke about communication more than most of my respondents. At the same time, many
of the themes they discussed—for instance, the "constant" nature of their
contact, the use of technology to facilitate interconnectedness, and the
way the distance "forced" them to communicate—reflected how other
commuters talked about staying in touch.

In this chapter, continuing on the theme of "apart togetherness," I look
at how respondents navigated their marriages from a distance. Drawing on
theoretical literature (e.g., Lefebvre [1991] 2014), I argue that commuter
spouses often privileged social and mental space over physical space. For
instance, many characterized the houses they shared with their partners as
"home," regardless of how much time they personally spent living there.
A major factor in their downplaying of physical distance was their ability
to remain in constant contact with their partners via various communication technologies (CTs). Commuter spouses recreated their in-person relationships through CTs, using different devices to convey different kinds
of information. Yet these technologies were not sufficient to bridge the
gap created by physical separation—a point that emerged in my respondents' discussions of health and childcare issues. I conclude the chapter by
discussing the implications of these findings beyond commuter spouses.
Because they live out such large portions of their relationships through
these technologies, commuters are in a strategic position to shed light on
our understanding of the dynamics and impact of CTs more generally.

Three Types of Space

In thinking about how commuter spouses managed their long-distance relationships, it is useful to consider three different types of space. For Henri
Lefebvre ([1991] 2014) and other theorists who have delineated between
these types, there is "social space" (the space in which social relations lie),
which is distinct from "mental (or 'cognitive') space" and from "physical

space" (289). Rather than being purely abstract, social space is "real" in the same sense that other "concrete abstractions" such as money are real (289). As Edward Soja (1989) points out, these three types of space "interrelate and overlap"; indeed, "both the material space of physical nature and the ideational space of human nature have to be seen as being socially produced and reproduced" (120). While Lefebvre was initially writing about space in terms of its role in the reproduction of capitalism, the general concept of these three notions of space is useful for thinking about how commuter spouses navigated their marriages.

In talking with commuters, I found that many of them were striving to keep consistency in their marriages—to "have a normal relationship" (to use Alexis's words) to the extent that it was possible, despite the physical distance. They continually asserted the importance of the social and cognitive aspects of their relationships with their partners (and, when applicable, children), and they highlighted the ability of these aspects to transcend physical separation.

Home Is Where the Spouse Is: The Importance of Social and Mental Space

As discussed further in appendix A, a majority of respondents were in "satellite" relationships, where one partner remained in the home that the couple had previously shared while the other moved for a job opportunity. One way that commuters underscored the significance of social and mental space was by describing their shared residences with their partners as "home," regardless of how much time they had personally spent living there. In fact, when asked how they thought about their two residences, more than three-fourths of respondents described at least one of the homes as "both of ours," while less than one-quarter (24%) agreed with "one is mine and one is my partner's."[2]

Moreover, among the respondents who thought of at least one residence as shared, 39 percent further downplayed their physical separation by indicating that they felt the other residence belonged to neither of them. Alexis, for instance, told me, "This is not home for me, in [this city], at all." She went on to explain, "My home's always where he's at, regardless of where we were at. Like when I was down in [another city during our first separation], I never made that my place. I never put money into it because that was not where I was gonna live. . . . It's just like college or something. You never call your dorm room your actual house. You always want to call your house where you identify yourself and where he's at."

Even though she lived in a house that she owned and not a dorm room, Alexis—like many commuter spouses—continued to think of her residence as temporary, and she stressed the symbolic importance of the living space that she and Jim shared. This concept of "home is where the spouse is" not only illustrates how commuters downplayed their current lack of physical proximity, but it also aligns with my discussion from the previous chapter. That is, it suggests the durability of notions about marital interdependence, even for these career-driven, ostensibly autonomous commuters.

Virtually Together: "Constant" Contact through CTs

When I was in my office in Nashville, and my husband in his office in New York, we would leave open the Google chat app and communicate periodically throughout the workday. During a single day in 2012, we chatted about our weekends, discussed the logistics of his upcoming visit to Nashville, talked about what we might have for lunch (then discussed how the lunch was), talked about our family and friends and the work we were completing that day, and went back and forth sending each other the lyrics of a TV theme song. Then we signed off, and I left the office for the day, making the walk back to the nearby apartment I shared with a roommate. Strangely, we were both still highly productive in our jobs.

One reason commuter spouses were able to privilege the social and mental spaces they shared with their partners, and to downplay the significance of their physical separation, was that they had the tools to accomplish this. Via communication technologies they were able to feel "together" in many ways, even when geographically they were not.

During periods of noncohabitation, most commuters spoke with their spouses by phone at least once a day. About 38 percent indicated that they generally talked by phone three or more times a day, while 20 percent typically spoke about twice a day, 23 percent spoke about once a day, and only about 19 percent spoke less than once a day.[3] Phone calls, texting, and email were the most frequently used mechanisms of communication. Video chatting, online chatting, and keeping in touch through social media were less important. (One respondent emphasized that she was "not even friends" with her husband on Facebook.) Hardly anyone used snail mail, except for a few respondents who mentioned sending occasional cards or postcards to their partners. In fact, the interview question about snail mail tended to generate chuckles. "That would be cute!" one respondent exclaimed, in response.

Perhaps more revealing than the number of times they talked to their partners was how so many commuters emphasized their ongoing stream of communication. For example, Josie, a professor in her early fifties who had been in a commuting relationship for the past six years, told me that she was in touch with her husband Abe "during our waking hours, *constantly*" (emphasis in original). I asked her how often they spoke on the phone:

> Josie: Daily, do you mean, or?
> *If it's daily, how often per day?*
> Josie: Oh, every two hours. [*laughs*] Cell phones, you know? He has an iPad, I have an iPad. We Facetime. I just Facetimed with him before I saw you. I've talked to him three times today and it's, what, 12:30 [p.m.]?

Many respondents, like Josie, used words like "constant," "continued," or "ongoing" to describe their communication with their spouses. For instance, Madison—a CEO in her mid-forties who was living with her husband after a period apart—also said that their contact had been "constant" while they were not living together. In addition, like other people I interviewed, she explained how the couple had used different CTs to share different types of information. Asked what the couple's most important form of contact was, Madison indicated that it was the phone, although she said that they used texting more often: "He's on conference calls or I'm in meetings, and he would just want to tell me [through a text], 'Hey, I'm here. I've made it here safe' if he was leaving early . . . Just so I would know that he was leaving, but he would know that I was in a meeting." Then, asked if she and her husband emailed while they were apart, she indicated, "That's how we took care of kind of administrative items. 'I'll forward this here.' 'Take care of this.' 'Take care of that.' 'Did you see the message about the thing at school?' 'Did you get the baseball game schedule?' That kind of stuff we would use email for. But more interpersonal kind of stuff would be texts or calls."

Commuters often used email as the vehicle for nonemotive, task-oriented kinds of communications. Email was "more business-related," as one respondent put it; he added, "It's, 'Don't forget to send a deposit in,' or we've been refinancing this apartment and the home, so there's lots of business stuff that we have to go back and forth with." In this way, respondents replicated their various types of in-person communications—in-depth and sustained, brief and to-the-point, emotional, instrumental—by parceling out different kinds of information into different technological buckets.

This finding provides an interesting coda to a longstanding discussion in the communications field about the extent to which these types of new technologies are best suited to facilitate "impersonal" or "interpersonal" communication, or some combination of both. When the internet was still in its infancy many communications scholars suggested that computer-mediated communication was best suited—or only suited (Dubrovsky, Kiesler, and Sethna 1991)—for practical, not emotive, correspondence. As Gerald Phillips and Gerald Santoro (1989) asserted, for instance, communication via computer placed limits on "consideration of irrelevant and interpersonal and theoretical issues by focusing attention on the process and content of problem-solving discussion" (152). To a certain extent, this way of viewing internet communication aligns with the perceptions of many commuter spouses—including those, quoted above, who characterized email as a way to handle "administrative items" and as "more business-related" than other forms of staying in touch.

More recently, however, scholars have pointed to the ability of CTs to facilitate emotional connectedness—a point that commuter spouses also illustrate. Joseph Walther (1996), for instance, has asserted that computer-mediated communication, in some contexts, holds the capacity "to become 'hyperpersonal,' that is, to exceed FtF [face-to-face] interpersonal communication" (5). To be clear, Walther explains that such technologies have "hyperpersonal" potential because of the internet's appealing capacity to offer selective presentations of self (2007), and thus a relational capacity exceeding face-to-face communications. Yet communication technologies seemed to enable "hyperpersonal" interactions for some commuter spouses in a different way—by facilitating ongoing connection because of these geographically separated spouses' senses of obligation to use them.

The notion of sorting various types of information into different buckets also dovetails with other research on new innovations in communication. Christian Licoppe (2004), for instance, has observed that different CTs have benefits for specific types of communications. For instance, an SMS (text message) could "be used to defuse a tense situation, reaffirming a form of connected presence" (153). Texts, like other new vehicles for communication, also reduce the "transaction costs" of initiating contact: "The proliferation of communication devices reinforces this tendency by allowing the actors to distribute their interaction across a wider range of interactional resources, and by diversifying the trade-offs that they are prompted to make" (153). Licoppe also points out that "the boundaries between absence and presence eventually get blurred" (136) through repeated, sustained engagement with such resources.

As the intersection with Licoppe's work here suggests, this aspect of commuter marriage also ties into a broader narrative about the reduced importance of physical copresence in the information age. In their 1978 book, *The Network Nation*, Starr Roxanne Hiltz and Murray Turoff predicted that an outcome of computer-mediated communications would be the removal of "time and distance barriers" ([1978] 1993, 8). "One consequence of our highly mobile and rapidly changing society," they mused, "is the more rapid disintegration of family and friendship ties than had been the case in simpler times" (204). Yet the authors had "optimistic hypotheses" (204) regarding the ability of these new technologies to help sustain and strengthen these ties. More recent scholarship has also picked up on this theme. British economist Frances Cairncross (1997), for example, has argued that technological advancements such as the internet and wireless phones have created a "death of distance" that "loosens the grip of geography"—without, however, eliminating it (5).[4]

As people who carry out relatively large portions of their relationships in separate physical spaces from their partners, commuter spouses and other long-distance couples are in a unique position to illustrate the benefits of CTs for sustaining intimate connections. Indeed, many of my respondents—who privileged the social and emotional aspects of their marriages, and emphasized the "constant" nature of their contact—seemed to be living out Hiltz and Turoff's specific prediction about the benefits of computer-mediated communications for families, as well as exemplifying the broader narrative about a "death of distance."

Ted and Ramona

Ted and Ramona had been married for either thirty-four or thirty-five years—there was a discrepancy in their responses. Both agreed, however, that they had been in a commuter relationship for the past seven. The couple lived relatively close together, compared to others in my sample, though traffic patterns in their region meant that travel times could vary widely. The trip between their residences could take anywhere from less than an hour to over two hours, depending upon the time of day. Ted typically made that drive, and the couple saw each other three or four days a week. Ted and Ramona had grown children who now lived out of the house.

A corporate executive in his mid-fifties, Ted told me that he and his wife sent "a lot" of emails back and forth, in addition to talking on the phone three to four times a day. Like other respondents, Ted used the words "constant" and "continued" at several points in his interview to underscore how often he and Ramona kept in touch. Also like other respondents, he used different devices for different types of communication, with email as the medium used for task-sharing: "The emails are not so much mushy, mushy emails. It's, 'What about this?' It's, I would say, to keep making progress on—one of our daughters is getting married in August; we have another that just got engaged. It's, 'What about this?' So we send a lot of emails as far as, 'Have you done this?' Or, 'Can you call this?' Or, 'We're having some contractors doing some work.' So we use email quite a bit. Probably a half dozen emails on a daily basis."

Like her husband, Ramona—who worked in an administrative position at a university—indicated that various technologies were useful for sustaining their communication over a distance. At several points in her interview, she referenced the normalcy of their relationship. For instance, when asked how she and Ted relied on each other, she said that they did so "in the usual ways that a married couple does." Ramona also pointed out that Ted "has always been very comfortable working really long hours," and now she was beginning to do that as well. Thus, she said, being apart physically did not necessarily reduce the amount of time the couple spent communicating. "We've always—I was used to him traveling," she explained. "We've always sort of been used to, that he might be away a couple of nights a week. So it wasn't a big hardship for me. I work usually one night a week and one night a week I'm usually on campus for something else. So several nights a week I'm not at home anyway. . . . [Living apart is] not a burden for us at this point."

Ted, similarly, emphasized their busy schedules. "We probably communicate, via different media, as much when we're apart as we would if we saw each other an hour or two or three every night," he told me.

These "different media" included email and the phone, but Ted and Ramona used other forms of communication as well. For example, Ted talked about playing an online Scrabble game with his wife:

> Ramona and I have two games going, so she'll play a word and then it gets passed over to me. So, again, I feel like doing that stuff—and I'm not a big game player but I don't consider that playing a game with my wife, I consider that interacting because you can send little messages when you're playing your word and stuff like that. That's one of the things I really enjoy at night when I'm sitting at the apartment. I hear the "ding" and she's played her Scrabble word and I get to be a little bit competitive, and we like to beat each other. . . . To me, that continued interaction is very important to keep your sanity when you're apart.

Finally, like some other respondents, Ted emphasized that he "probably wouldn't" be living apart from his spouse were these technologies not available. "If this was the old days . . . and you had to use the rotary telephone to dial up and call, I probably would hate what I am doing," he told me. A few minutes after that, when we had moved on to a different topic, he paused mid-speech. "I just got an email from my wife," he said, "if you want to know for your record."

"Simple Talk" and Shared Leisure: Divergence from Earlier Research

As Ted and Ramona illustrate, communication technologies served a few different functions in these relationships. One of these functions was to facilitate commuter spouses' interdependence. As demonstrated in the previous chapter through the example of Art relying on his wife for "tech support," many respondents emphasized how various technologies enabled them to engage with their spouses in the collective management of tasks. This aspect of my respondents' experience sets them apart from the subjects of older research on commuter marriage. Prior work on this topic, much of which is based on research from the 1970s and 1980s, details challenges of staying in touch that may now seem antiquated—for example, the high cost of long-distance phone calls (Gerstel and Gross 1984, 57). Another issue with the phone, according to Gerstel and Gross in their 1984 study, was that it necessitated "constant exchanges" (57). "One must keep up one's side of the conversation," they explained (57). As Licoppe suggests above, technologies such as texting and email provide alternatives that promote the sense of "continuous presence" while at the same time not requiring constant, sustained interaction; thus, they lessen the "transaction costs" of these exchanges (2004, 153).

My respondents had available to them cell phones for talking and texting, email, instant messages, and video chat. With the push of some buttons or with a few keystrokes, they were able to check in to coordinate children's schedules or to make sure one of them was paying the month's utility bill online. They had the capacity, theoretically, to be reachable at almost any time, so that they could rely on each other—emotionally, financially, and logistically.

Yet another way commuter spouses used CTs was, simply, to talk. In their 1984 study, Gerstel and Gross observed that commuter spouses "experience the reduction in simple talk as a serious loss" (54). As one respondent told them, "I miss the opportunity to share the everyday things like 'what did you have for lunch today?' " (54). On the contrary, my respondents were equipped with the mechanisms for simple talk; in fact, two separate people (not married to each other) told me they would text their spouses about what they had eaten for lunch. Alexis and Jim chatting about groceries over Facetime and Ted and Ramona sending each other "little messages" about their Scrabble game were just two examples of how commuter spouses incorporated "simple talk" into their communications. One respondent mentioned being able to walk down the street and chat with his son, who lived with his spouse, about last night's Yankees game. Another said she had texted her husband earlier that day because she broke a vase—just to let him know what a klutz he had married. Many such examples emerged over the course of my interviews.

The commuters in my sample also used CTs to engage in leisure activities. This, too, was something that was lacking among commuter spouses in some prior studies. Gerstel and Gross found that one downside of living apart, for the couples in their 1984 sample, was the loss of shared leisure time. Commuters "are unable to share many planned leisure activities when they live apart" (60), they observed. For instance, one respondent told the researchers, "If I wanted to go to a movie, I wouldn't go there by myself . . . I don't get out a whole lot these days" (60). Today, commuter spouses can share activities remotely, and they do not necessarily have to "get out" to do it.[5] In fact, my respondents often highlighted their ability to engage in leisure activities they might otherwise do together while coresiding—for example, playing Xbox together online, or "movie nights" in which they watched the same films in their respective residences while chatting about them over the phone or online.

The differences between my findings and earlier research on this topic suggest that new technologies have reduced some of the challenges that would otherwise exist within these relationships. Indeed, some of my interviewees—those who had lived apart for long stretches or had lived apart earlier in their relationships and were doing it again now—explicitly indicated that new CTs had positively impacted their experiences of being in commuter marriages. For instance, one respondent who had previously lived apart from her husband around the time Gerstel and Gross were writing said the difference was that this time, "sometimes it felt like he wasn't even really gone." She mused, "I wondered if we were even that good of a couple to interview because there was a lot of flexibility with his schedule and we were in constant contact."

It is also possible that, because of these technological advances, commuter spouses are a different population now. That is, some types of people who never would have considered commuting in the past may now be more likely to contemplate that option. In fact, some of my respondents, like Ted, as we have seen, explicitly indicated that they likely would not have made the decision to live apart had these technologies not been available. Alexis told me, for instance, "If there weren't cell phones and stuff like that—if there were only landlines—I probably would have made the choice to have just stayed home." In short, these respondents viewed CTs as instrumental in reducing the impact of geographic separation. By privileging social and mental space, and by keeping in touch virtually, they reduced the strain created by physical distance.

Not Being There: Can Technology Bridge Physical Space?

Some commuter spouses were more adept than others at using the mechanisms of communication they had available. As explored in the previous chapter, some respondents indicated that the distance actually improved their communication with each other, as it forced them to remain in touch about both practical and emotional matters on an ongoing basis. Yet other respondents suggested the reverse.[6]

Technology could potentially reduce the impact of distance and make commuter marriages easier. However, for most, it could not fully bridge the gap of physical separation. The commuter lifestyle presented many challenges that could not all be met by "constant contact" over email, text, phone calls, and other mechanisms. For one thing, the bureaucratic infrastructure in the United States today is still organized for married couples who live together. For that reason, marital noncohabitation creates logistical issues that cannot be resolved in the virtual world. Some respondents, for instance, discussed their problems with getting insurance or mortgages on two "primary" residences for one married couple.

Moreover, while emphasizing how often they communicated with their spouses, many respondents still suggested that CTs were not a substitute for in-person contact. Perhaps the most obvious potential issue was the reduced time for sex and other forms of physical intimacy, as discussed in chapter 1. But my interviewees described other issues with being in touch through CTs as well, such as feeling disconnected, not being able to adequately convey emotions, and a lack of resolution at the end of arguments. Asked what he liked least about living apart from his wife, one respondent in his mid-twenties told me, "Oh, just the aloneness of trying to share emotions over the phone or through an email . . . [Y]ou don't get the emotion when you're trying to talk to somebody on the phone. It's easy to kind of wall yourself off from the situation you're in on the other end of the phone. . . . So what I liked least was the inability of trying to share the emotions that we wanted to. It was just difficult to convey them through some of the mediums we used to communicate."

One salient theme that emerged among the women I interviewed was that their husbands had more difficulty than they did in communicating over the phone—a point the husbands themselves tended to support. For example, Mae, a professor in her late thirties who had resumed living with her spouse by the time I interviewed her, told me:

> With our communication styles, [my husband] is not a super verbal person and that was really hard for me. And I've been the kind of person, especially at the time, when I need to talk through problems, and I need assurance—especially verbal assurance—that if there's a problem, that everything's really okay. And if you're living with someone, there's more space to talk about that, or you can pick up on someone's bodily language or cues, that, "Okay, everything's all right. There's no tension here." But that's gone when you're communicating via phone or email. So I found that that was the hardest part of our relationship.

Mae also emphasized that conflict resolution was more difficult over a distance:

> Like, you can say on the phone, "Okay, everything's fine." Even if I'm wrong and I'm sorry, blah blah blah. But then you just get off the phone, and that's kind of it. If you're with someone in person, you can really feel when the tension is lifted and that person's moved on and if everything's quote-unquote "okay," but you just don't have that when you're living apart. . . . And so for me what I would do, and I know my husband didn't appreciate this, is that I would then call him back, like, "Well, we need to—I don't feel good about this." And he would say, "I told you everything's fine." Like, "I'm not upset about this," or whatever. But for me, I really needed the in-person communication to feel better about it if there was a conflict. . . . I think that was, besides missing him, the hardest thing about living apart.

Like Mae, other respondents talked about their difficulties dealing with lingering tension while they were apart from their spouses. If you are not physically with your partner, as Aviva explained, "It's impossible to actually end an argument." Comments like Mae's and Aviva's resonate with prior research on the potential pitfalls of CTs for long-distance relationships. Wilding (2006), for instance, characterizes email and other communication methods as "sunny day" technologies for the transnational families in her sample (134): "They provide few opportunities for engaging in the personal care that is sometimes required by ageing parents, or for negotiating the conflicts and crises that can erupt as a result of continued interactions" (134–135).[7] My respondents, too, suggested that CTs were key to their everyday pleasant and even mundane interactions, but that these technologies could not always adequately substitute for copresence, particularly during—and in the aftermath of—unpleasant conversations.

Wilding's finding that continued contact through such technologies could actually create "conflicts and crises" was borne out in my research as well. Some commuters told me that the availability of CTs created wrinkles in their relationships. One respondent in his mid-fifties, who had been married for twenty years and living apart from his wife for the last few, explained that expectations surrounding communication could become problematic: "Between email, texting, and cell phone conversations—I guarantee you there will be times there will be twenty messages between the combination of all three. Very rare for a day to go by—no, there is no such thing as a day without communication. If there was, there would be a crisis and there would be fear. That, 'What happened? Why didn't you call? Why didn't you email?' . . . The communication's almost constant. . . . Sometimes I will call her in the middle of one of her quote-unquote 'shows,' and she will want to watch a TV show instead of talking to me. And that will make me angry." Later in the interview, he added, "What's happened is, because communication is so easy with all of these different mediums, if I don't hear from her, I'll get worried. Like, why hasn't she emailed?"

As responses like these illustrate, while many commuters spoke positively about how "constant" communication could help to bridge their geographic distance, the availability of communication technologies also produced some relationship challenges. I have discussed how commuter spouses viewed their marriages through the lenses of both individualism and interdependence. Generally, respondents framed interconnectedness as a positive thing; however, these findings suggest that interconnectedness could be stressful for commuter couples as well.

"It Beat the Crap Outta Me": Physical Distance and Health Concerns

Toward the end of my fellowship, I had a miscarriage. Technically, it was a "missed" miscarriage. For several weeks, it was unclear whether the pregnancy was still viable, and I had to have my blood taken every three days to check my HCG levels. This proved bureaucratically fraught, as I was traveling back and forth to Nashville over that period, finalizing the upcoming national conference that would be the capstone of my fellowship. Finding a doctor who is not your primary physician, in a different city, to take your blood—even when you work at a research university connected to a major medical center—is oddly difficult. I contacted the university health center, to no avail, and frantically called local physicians. Could I take the blood myself and airmail it to my physician? Could I throw myself at the mercy of a drug testing lab? I began to feel that I was the star of a bad Rodney Dangerfield skit: "Take My Blood: Please!" Finally, a sympathetic colleague drove me to her doctor's office and advocated for me. The doctor was able to coordinate with mine, and they passed my records back and forth via email. Eventually, I needed to have a procedure done, and for that I waited until I returned to New York after the conference. I wanted to do it in my doctor's office, with my husband there.

Some of my respondents fared worse than I did. In two couples, the husbands developed serious health issues during the commuting periods of their marriages. Mark, for instance, whom I describe in chapter 4 as being generally extremely positive about commuter marriage, indicated that the frequent plane trips across the country to see his wife had impacted him physically. Asked, "Is there anything you didn't like about living apart?," he replied, "Oh, yeah! The travel sucked. Y'know, there were times I was very lonely. . . . And, y'know, having such [a] physical challenge can get an enormous toll on you. I mean, it really affected my health. The stroke was directly attributable to airplane travel. . . . The trick was not to think about it while you're doin' it. Right? . . . But when you're done, you realize, 'Holy shit, y'know. It beat the crap outta me.'"

Jay, too, developed a serious condition during the time he lived apart from his wife, Sophie. Jay and Sophie—professors who had previously lived a plane ride apart but had resumed cohabitating by the time I interviewed them—both spoke about his illness in their interviews. "It was terrible," Jay told me, "I mean, I was very, very sick physically . . . to the point where we were almost breaking, the marriage." Sophie directly attributed the worsening of her husband's condition to their commuting arrangement. "You know, had I been there, we would have kind of had the wherewithal to say like, 'Hey, you should see a doctor, you know, you have to get this checked out,'" she told me, "but I think there was something about like my coming and going, everything just felt so, like you know, like we were barely hanging on and you know and I'd say, 'Oh, I think you should go see a doctor!' and he'd say, 'Yeah, I think you're right.' [*Laughs*] And somehow it wouldn't happen."

Sophie's account suggests that one pitfall of commuting, potentially, is that the spouses are not physically together long enough to mutually address issues as they arise. In my instance, I felt I needed to wait until I was finished with my conference and back home with my husband to schedule my medical procedure. For some commuters, as for Sophie and me, the arrangement was a bit like treading water in this sense.

While the two couples I have discussed in this section were dealing with extreme health concerns, other respondents also described various, somewhat more minor health problems that either originated with, or were exacerbated by, the strain of travel. They talked about the physical toll on their bodies of spending so much time in cars, on trains, and hurtling through the air in pressurized cabins, as well as the mental toll of living separately. Their descriptions resonated with other accounts of commuting relationships. A *Washington Post* article on Ted and Heidi Cruz's commuter marriage, for example, discusses how Heidi battled depression during their geographic separation (Harlan 2016). It is also important to note that I did not ask respondents specifically about the health consequences of commuting; perhaps more of these accounts would have arisen if I had broached the topic. Regardless, my interviewees suggested that, while communication technologies could partially bridge physical distance, they did not replace in-person visits. Further, the act of traveling to see each other could take a toll on commuters' bodies as they moved through physical space.

Are the Kids All Right? Child-Rearing, Apart

One place where both the capacities and the shortcomings of CTs were particularly prominent was in respondents' discussions about their children. My interviewees gave rich accounts of the various ways in which they used technologies to stay in touch with their kids while living elsewhere. I heard stories about chatting on cell phones in airports, Facetiming with astounded toddlers, and texting teenagers from the office. Further, when commuter spouses who had children discussed their virtual reliance on each other, collective child-rearing was a major element of that discussion. Commuters used technologies to check in with each other about their children's well-being, to coordinate kids' schedules, to pay for extracurricular activities, to look at grades, and to engage in numerous other collective parenting tasks. CTs, in short, played a critical role in co-parenting over a distance.

At the same time, the inability of CTs to fully compensate for physical absence was perhaps most obvious in respondents' discussions about child-rearing. Indeed, many parents in my sample said that having children profoundly complicated the dynamics of their arrangements, despite everyone's access to multiple mechanisms of contact. Some interviewees without children spontaneously mentioned that they wouldn't have undertaken this lifestyle if they had been parents. For example, one respondent, when asked whether she had any children, replied, "Oh God, no," adding, "Do people really do this with kids?"

Commuters who did have kids, moreover, tended to either indicate, or at least ponder, the potential damage the arrangement was doing to their children. The following is a selection of such responses:

> Sometimes I would say, "Is it worth it?" You can never recover that lost time with your kids on those key events or key activities.
>
> [My eight-year-old son] may have some anger issues toward me. Not anything that manifests itself in school, but, I mean, when we're play wrestling, he's slugging me. He's not wrestling.
>
> My children, they really needed [my husband]. I think they suffered because of that. For sure, my son really, really suffered. They suffered from depression and also just suffered because they missed him. . . . I think it was really unfair to my children to have to go through that.

Another respondent told me that both her husband and son "cried every week" when it came time for her husband to leave. Interestingly, she said that while her spouse had not engaged in a lot of "hands-on childcare" when he previously worked from home, his physical absence was now consequential in his son's life: "My son was just really affected by the fact that dad wasn't just in the office upstairs. I'm like, 'How can you tell the difference?' It's like just his presence gave my son security that I didn't realize was necessary."

As suggested by this respondent, my interviewees particularly stressed the importance of physical copresence when it came to childrearing. However, commuters' worries about the impact of this lifestyle on their children seemed to exist on a spectrum. Some were intensely concerned for their children, others suggested that there were perhaps some negative repercussions, while yet others were not sure about the consequences, if any, of this lifestyle on their children. One interviewee, for instance, said she did not know if the commuting arrangement was best for the kids in the long run. "There's not a book for this," she observed. She paused and added, "Well, I guess there's going to be now."

Unfortunately, this is still not that book. To be clear, I am not a psychologist or family therapist, nor did I interview any commuter children. Whether the children of commuter spouses experience any durable negative repercussions is beyond the scope of both my analysis here and my overall expertise. I can assert that many commuter parents I interviewed were at least somewhat concerned about the impact on their kids, and some—like the ones quoted above—explicitly stated that they felt the arrangement had been harmful to their children. Other research has indicated, similarly, that commuting parents describe feelings of guilt about being separated from their kids (Johnson 1987; Rotter, Barnett, and Fawcett 1998). Journalistic accounts—such as former Hillary Clinton advisor Anne-Marie Slaughter's now-iconic piece in *The Atlantic*, "Why Women Still Can't Have It All" (July/August 2012)—have also detailed the stresses of commuter parenthood and its perceived impact on children. Moreover, while little scholarship has focused directly on children's experiences in these situations, one study found that, across three African-American commuter families, the kids expressed concerns such as feeling "left out," feeling like the commuting parent was "uninvolved" in their lives, and feeling "anger" when that parent was not present during their important life events (Jackson, Brown, and Patterson-Stewart 2000, 29–30).

Yet some of my respondents also suggested that their living arrangements had impacted their kids positively. For example, some felt it had increased their children's self-reliance. "I think it was probably good for [my son], to tell you the truth," one commuter parent told me, for example, continuing: "You know, not to have two parents all over him."

Others pointed out that, through this arrangement, their children had "learned to be independent" and to "take care of themselves." These responses demonstrate that some commuter spouses embraced the cultural value of individualism not only for themselves but for their offspring as well.[8]

In sum, while many commuter spouses emphasized the deficiencies of CTs as a substitute for their continued physical presence in their children's lives, there was diversity in how these couples interpreted the overall impact of their living arrangements on their children.

Outliers

Some respondents, more than others, emphasized the impact of their geographic separation on their marriages and families. Those who felt more of an impact tended to be the people who lived further apart from each other, who saw each other less frequently, and who had fewer opportunities for spontaneous moments of contact. For instance, Wade, who worked in the technology sector and lived in a time zone fifteen hours apart from his wife, explained that it was difficult for the couple to coordinate their phone calls: "One of the bigger challenges is because of the time difference, one or the other of us tends to be at work. And when you are, it's so easy to get distracted. 'Oh, I'll just glance over emails while I'm chatting away' or something. There are definitely times when she calls me out on, 'Oh, you're doing something else.' Which I feel bad about, but sometimes it's the only way to squeeze in a call."

Additionally, there were other respondents who did not participate in the narrative of "constant" contact, indicating that communicating often was not their personal preference. "My wife's not a big phone person," one interviewee told me, adding, "*I'm* not a terribly big phone person . . . I think a lot of couples sort of check in with each other a few times during the day. We just don't do that" (emphasis in original). As discussed in chapter one, I found that most commuter spouses emphasized both the interconnectedness and the individualism in their marriages, with some outliers living at the tails of the "interconnected" curve. This finding extended to how they talked about distance and communication.

A Caveat

The above respondent's comment that he did not speak to his wife frequently on the phone, but not because he was unable to (rather, because they "just don't do that"), illustrates one way that the findings in this chapter may not be applicable to some other types of relationships. The commuters in my sample generally had access to CTs in ways that other types of long-distance couples do not. Deployed military spouses are perhaps the most obvious counterexample. In their work on FIFO couples, further, Barbara Pini and Robyn Mayes (2012) point out that the availability and usefulness of communication technologies can vary widely in these relationships. "Some women talk of only being able to communicate with their partners by satellite phone," they explain, "which means calls tend to be very brief and often end without warning" (76). Wilding (2006) similarly reported that access to communication technologies was an issue for some of the transnational migrants in her study.

My respondents were people who, while often quite busy, theoretically *could* be in touch with their partners when they wanted to be. They had that option. Most of them worked in white-collar office jobs in major urban or suburban areas of the United States. They were not isolated in combat areas or out on oil rigs without access to phones. Thus, their narratives about "constant" contact were in some ways specific to their situation. And life may have been easier for them in this respect; indeed, prior research has found that the ability to communicate verbally is a key coping mechanism for long-distance couples (Holt and Stone 1988). At the same time, while this aspect of their experience distinguishes my respondents from other kinds of living-apart couples (as well as the commuter spouses in some earlier studies), it also renders them a particularly illuminating group. Today's commuter marriages are a strategic site for understanding the benefits and pitfalls of CTs because these spouses *do* use these devices with such regularity.

Conclusions

As discussed in the previous chapter, commuter spouses still rely on each other while apart, in a multiplicity of ways. Because they have such broad access to CTs, and because they live out such comparatively large portions of their relationships through these mechanisms, commuter spouses are key figures within the larger story about the "death of distance" (Cairncross 1997). Indeed, the people I interviewed were able to overcome distance—to some extent—by privileging social and emotional space over the physical space between them, and by relying on CTs to temper the impact of their separation. Specifically, they replicated their in-person relationships by assigning different types of information to different communications "buckets."[9] Some were even able to use these technologies to facilitate a kind of "hyperpersonal" (Walther 1996) interaction that might not otherwise have existed between them.

Still, while my findings in this chapter contribute to literature about the declining importance of geography, they also demonstrate that technology cannot (currently) fully transcend physical space. Distance was not "dead" for these couples. It still mattered.

Commuters' narratives about staying in touch not only shed light on the dynamics of these marriages, but they also reflect how so many of us now sustain our intimate relationships through CTs when the demands of work and family preclude physical togetherness. The use of technology to bridge physical space, but its inability to do so fully, likely resonates with other types of couples who rely on CTs—for example, couples who work long hours or maintain incompatible schedules. New technologies can help geographically separate individuals to manage tasks together, but they are not a panacea. One study of divorced coparents, for instance, found that such emergent technologies could facilitate joint planning and decision-making—but not always, especially if the coparent relationship was contentious (Ganong et al. 2012). Regardless of their limitations, these technologies are not just coping mechanisms for spouses who live in two different residences but are integral parts of life now for all types of families.

Indeed, in the time I have spent working on this chapter from my home office, just today, my nanny has texted me photos of my baby in music class, I have had email exchanges with colleagues, students, and my TAs, my mother has called to thank me for a birthday gift, I have responded to some comments on Facebook, and I have instant-messaged with my husband to plan dinner.

Looking ahead, additional advancements in technology are almost certainly in store for future generations of commuter spouses. While my research extends the story begun by scholars several decades ago, it is not the final chapter. Other forms of technology that currently exist, such as video chat, may become more widespread. Given my respondents' concerns about lack of bodily cues and about sharing emotions, it is interesting that Skype and other forms of video chat were not more popular among these commuters.[10] In fact, when asked, "What would you say is the most important form of communication through which you stay in touch with your partner when you're apart?" only two respondents said that it was Facetime, one replied "phone and Skype" and indicated that she could not decide between the two, and one said it was a "close tie" between phone and email. Everyone else said that it was the phone.

Perhaps one reason for the relative lack of emphasis on video chat was that, though they can be helpful, these somewhat recent technologies also present their own issues. For instance, those commuters who had used Skype tended to discuss its glitches. Describing the platform as "kind of a pain in the neck," one interviewee recalled, "When I first got my iPad, we were Skyping for a little bit but it doesn't seem worth it. You know, the syncing is always off and the voice is different from the image, and you gotta sit there in front of it, whereas when we talk [on the phone] I have my little headphones and I'm walking around the apartment or I'm walking outside. So we do Skype but rarely."

On the other hand, when respondents discussed Facetime specifically, it was mainly to point out its benefits. To return to the example from the beginning of this chapter of Alexis and Jim, who grocery shopped "together" via Facetime, Alexis told me that Facetime had been "great" for their relationship. The first time she and Jim had lived apart, she explained, "It kinda sucked because you're always on the phone, but now with like iPads and Facetiming it's—not like you're there, but it's pretty good."

In their 1984 book, Gerstel and Gross argued that commuter spouses problematized the assumption that "all primary groups require daily face-to-face interaction in order to function" (15). Yet, in the present day, the concept of "face-to-face interaction" has become a bit hazier. Commuter spouses could have "face-to-face" contact in a sense through these technologies, if they desired. Still, most preferred the phone. To put this finding in perspective, Apple released Facetime in 2010, and I conducted interviews in 2012 and 2013. The technology was so relatively new that I did not include a question about it specifically on my interview schedule.

Instead, I asked about "video chat (like Skype)." It is likely that not all of my respondents had access to Facetime, or were adept at using it.

It remains to be seen whether Facetime and future advancements will revolutionize the commuter relationship. In 1937, sociologist Howard Odum coined the term "technicways": the concept that new technological advances can subsequently "modify human behavior and institutions as to outmode the earlier, natural rate of societal evolution" (337). However, according to Odum, there is typically a delay between the introduction of the technology and broadscale social change. Perhaps what we are seeing with these commuters is simply this "cultural lag" (Odum 1953, 204) before video-based communication begins to normatively pattern human behavior. As technologies with video components become more widespread, accessible, user-friendly, and generally less of a "pain in the neck" (to borrow my respondent's words), they may become instrumental in helping these spouses navigate their geographic distance. On the other hand, some commuters suggested that such technologies simply were not appealing to them. As one woman explained, "I don't feel like I need to *see* [my husband]. I'm not sure what Skype would add . . . I haven't felt this moment where I'm like, 'I really wanna Skype him.' I'll just call him [on the phone]" (emphasis in original).

Finally, while in this chapter I have focused on commuter spouses' emphases on social and mental space, and on their use of CTs, I should note that respondents also attempted to manage their physical space in various ways. That is, they also strove to overcome the demands of separation by gaining specific expertise. They told me about memorizing flight schedules and navigating airports. They knew which GPS apps accounted for traffic, which routes were ideal, and they knew when to begin their drive and when there would be traffic. They told me about which part of the train to sit in, and about how to find out before anyone else which track your train would be arriving on, so you could beat the last-minute surge of the crowd.[11] Through these mechanisms, commuter spouses gained a sense of control over physical space. When it came to how they got into these relationships, on the other hand, they often felt a lack of control—a topic I explore in the next chapter.

3

Nobody's Decision

The "Choice" to Live Apart

Dawn and Al

Dawn was talking about money. When I asked her, "Would you say that you live apart because of financial necessity?," she replied, "Yeah. Well—yeah. Well . . ." Then she paused and added, "They're all such complicated questions, aren't they? Because originally, I would say it was out of financial necessity, because we knew we needed a second income. Or wanted a second income. Because that's part of the issue is, what is necessity? Could we have gotten by on one income? Probably. I knew I *wanted* to work" (emphasis in original).

A fifty-four-year-old academic, Dawn had been married to Al for twenty-nine years, and they had been living apart for nine by the time I interviewed them. Dawn, who had moved away to a house in a different state, was typically the one who made the three-hour drive back and forth to visit her husband in their shared family home. The couple saw each other a few days a week during the academic year and were together over school breaks and the summer, though Dawn also traveled during that time for various consulting projects. Their three children, now adults, had been teens when Dawn began commuting. The couple had also recently purchased another home abroad, and Dawn joked (I think) about fleeing the country for good if Obama did not get reelected.

Asked the same question about financial necessity, Al—who worked at a university in a nonteaching role—was a bit more definitive about the mechanisms behind their arrangement. "No. No—Well, no," he responded. "It's more in terms of, she had the job. Practically speaking, she had to be there. We could have, I think—Well, we lived on one salary for a long time. There was no reason why we couldn't have continued to do that. But it was more like, this is her professional—this is her career. And this is just what needs to happen."

Most respondents, like Dawn and Al, did not interpret financial need as the only factor, or even a primary factor, in their noncohabitation. These commuter spouses, who indicated that living apart was a necessity, but not a financial one per se, viewed their career pursuits as crucial for reasons beyond remuneration. Al's comment, for instance, framing noncohabitation as something the couple "had to" do, echoed the nonagentic language of many other respondents. The individuals in my sample—predominantly white, well-educated, and relatively high-earning—were people whom we would expect to have (relative) access to options when it came to their careers and family lives. Yet they often suggested they lacked choices.

This chapter explores their nonagentic narrative and the mechanisms behind it. Framing noncohabitation as a form of "deviance," I address the question: if my interviewees were not driven by economic necessity, how did they account for their perceived lack of choice about entering into these nonnormative relationships? In response, I suggest that my respondents' perceptions of strain were the result of a concatenation of factors, including a capitalist system influencing individual conceptions of choice, highly specialized professional labor markets, and strong investment in career identity. At the same time, commuters were also driven by collectivist aims; many viewed their lifestyle as a necessary investment that would benefit their family in the long run. In addition to extending our understanding of the utility of a deviance framing more generally, the findings in this chapter enhance our understanding of professional identity development in the postindustrial economy as well as highlighting the disjuncture between the contemporary structure of professional work and conventional family life.

A Note on Terminology: "Deviance"

Throughout this chapter, I use the term "deviance" when discussing commuter spouses' atypical marital arrangements. I use the term in the way that social scientists have historically used it: to denote deviation from a norm, not as a concept having any subjective, moral implications. I use it interchangeably with "nonnormativity"—also a purely descriptive, sociological term.

I argue that despite their deviance—and, in some ways, because of it—commuter spouses are uniquely poised to shed light on the dynamics of professional work more generally. In this sense, my analysis in this chapter is in line with the original spirit of the sociology of deviance, which sought to analyze nonnormative behavior in order to better understand broader social structures and processes (Epstein 1994).[1]

Is This Normal? Commuter Spouses, Stigma, and Deviance

About four months prior to my touchdown in Nashville, when I was initially offered the fellowship at Vanderbilt, I balked. It was a fairly well paying two-year gig working on an interesting project with a senior scholar whose work I respected. It was also a two-hour plane ride from New York. When I discussed my dilemma with other academics, they were often confused. Although my colleagues knew that my husband would remain at his job (and it is important to note that at the time I had no children), they seemed to take for granted that I would pursue the new opportunity and we would live apart for the two years. They seemed to view this as the inevitable next step for me—not as a choice or a decision to be made.

Like any social science nerd facing a personal problem, I began to view the reactions of other people as data. Specifically, as a scholar of deviance, I was interested in their casual attitudes toward the concept of two spouses not living together. I was already somewhat familiar with the literature on the "two-body problem" of partners who are both academics and striving to hit the work/family jackpot: positions in the same geographic location. But in the reactions of other academics, I saw something more than recognition that this problem was fairly commonplace. I began to wonder whether living apart from one's partner had become a default expectation within my profession—and perhaps in other contexts as well. Was commuter marriage still deviant, or had it become normalized?

I understand why some might be opposed to interpreting commuter spouses as "deviant." My own experience as a commuter spouse seemed to suggest that these types of relationships had become routine, at least in academia. Further, my respondents were relatively well-educated (mainly) white people in professional careers and heterosexual marriages—people who, at first glance, may seem highly integrated within society and, in many respects, pretty "normal." We might resist lumping them into a category of scholarship with others whose behavior may appear more "objectively" nonnormative—for instance, criminals, men who have sexual encounters with others in public restrooms (Humphreys 1975), alcoholics (Rubington 1975), substance users and abusers (e.g., Akers et al. 1979), or even women who work as dominatrices, about whom I have written previously (Lindemann 2012).

On the other hand, scholars have long called for an expansion of the study of deviance to include nonnormative behavior within all socioeconomic groups. They have reasoned that focusing solely on "underdogs" and leaving out "updogs" results in a classist and potentially exclusionary definition of what constitutes nonnormative behavior (Herman-Kinney and Kinney 2013, drawing on Goffman [1963] 2009; Liazos 1972). Recognizing the importance of studying nonnormativity at all rungs of the social ladder, for instance, researchers have explored various forms of "high class" (Passas 1990) deviance, such as that which takes place within the upper echelons of government and corporations (Robinson and Murphy 2009; Simon and Eitzen 2002).

Though relatively privileged, commuter spouses may be considered "deviant" in several respects. First, in order to achieve their career goals, they enter into relationships that are not typical. Indeed, the commuter lifestyle inherently resists a dominant cultural narrative. As other scholars have pointed out (e.g., Stafford 2005), the concept of a shared residence underlies cultural assumptions about family in the United States.

For instance, the U.S. Census uses a definition of "family" that assumes coresidence and has remained unchanged since 1930 (Pemberton 2015).[2] Commuter spouses remain a statistical minority as well. Recall that Murray-Close found that even among spouses with doctorates—who are relatively likely to live apart—the prevalence of noncohabitation in 2000 was only 2.9 percent for men and 3.5 percent for women (Murray-Close 2013). Further, this figure includes spouses who lived apart for all reasons, not simply work-related factors. Commuter spouses, as Murray-Close (2013) puts it, are "unusual but not unknown" (2).

In addition to their statistical deviance, these noncohabitating spouses are deviant in the sense that they engage in nonnormative behavior that puts them at risk for "spoiled" identity (Goffman [1963] 2009). That is, they may experience stigma when others find out about their lifestyle (Magnuson and Norem 1999). Indeed, earlier research on these couples focused on social disapproval. In her 1985 book, for instance, Winfield observed, "Commuters, because of the negative response of others, are frequently almost secretive about their living together, apart, arrangement" (86), though she predicted that as the lifestyle became more common, "there will be fewer raised eyebrows from significant others" (86).

Winfield's prediction has been realized to some extent. Some scholars question whether society has become more accepting of these lifestyles since these earlier studies were completed (e.g., Bergen 2010a, 49). As discussed in this book's introduction, there are now high-profile examples of such relationships and even self-help books focused on how to navigate these arrangements. Moreover, the sense among the commuters I interviewed—particularly the ones who had been living apart for decades and thus had a longitudinal perspective—was that this lifestyle has become more widely accepted. While I did not directly assess changes in the acceptability of commuter marriage over time, based on what we know about shifting gender roles and labor markets, and the fact that this lifestyle has likely increased in prevalence (Brooke 2006), I would imagine that commuter marriage is more normalized today than it was in the mid-1980s.

Yet it still holds a stigma. Further, recent research suggests that this social disapproval is likely gendered. Communication studies scholar Karla Mason Bergen (2010), for instance, found that commuter wives experienced judgment and felt the need to excuse and to justify their marriages to others (see also Bergen, Kirby, and McBride 2007; M. Holmes 2004b). The gendered dimension of this stigma likely sets commuter spouses apart from some other types of long-distance couples. Army wives, for instance, may more easily fit into a broader narrative about women's place being in the home and supporting their husbands' careers (Gassmann 2010; Harrell 2003). Along the same lines, based on an analysis of postings made on an online chat forum mainly for women married to men working in FIFO arrangements in the mining industry in Australia, Pini and Mayes (2012) found that patriarchal relations were replicated in these families. Stigma and judgment from others were not discussed as major themes—if they even appeared at all. Commuter spouses, on the other hand, seem to encounter a unique stigma because the woman's career is a major factor in the separation. (I further discuss the gendered dynamics of these relationships in the next two chapters.)

My interviewees discussed stigmatization in ways that resonated with prior research on commuter marriage. A majority of my respondents (n=64; 66%) indicated that they had been judged negatively for adopting this lifestyle.[3] The gendered aspects of this stigma were also visible among my interviewees, with 85% of women respondents (n=51) indicating that they had experienced such judgment, compared to only 35% (n=13) of men. Josie, for instance, told me that she received critiques from family members more often than her husband did: "The only thing that he'll get is, 'Why doesn't [Josie] quit her job and live with you?'" Quinn, a sports coach in her late twenties, similarly spoke to the gendered dimensions of social disapproval, telling me, "You get the classics that drive me absolutely insane, which are, you know, that I'm not being a good wife 'cause I'm not being supportive and following my husband."

College professors like Dawn, moreover, did not seem to escape stigmatization, as the following exchange illustrates:

> *Do you find that there are people in your life who challenge or don't understand the fact that you live apart?*
>
> Dawn: Lots. But I would say that certainly there were more in the beginning. People have kind of come to accept our relationship and the way it's developed and our living situation. But even now, there are folks who just don't get it. And don't believe in it. And do still challenge us and challenge the veracity of the relationship. 'How good of a relationship can you have when you don't live together?' Challenge the damage that might be done to our relationship by not living together.

Notably, academics in my sample were no less likely than other respondents to indicate that they had experienced judgment for their lifestyle. As in the case of Dawn and Al, however, this judgment more often came from their family and friends than other academics. (This was the case for me as well.) One professor, for instance, told me that her mother-in-law questioned the fact that she and her spouse lived apart, "but none of our friends thought it was odd, because most of our friends were also in academia and kind of understand sometimes what you need to do." Another respondent, who also worked in academia, described an experience strikingly similar to mine, emphasizing that noncohabitation had been "normalized" in this profession: "I was genuinely surprised at the extent to which other people, more than even I was ready to initially when I was exploring this, really normalized it for me. They would—everyone would either describe some period where they went through a similar arrangement or someone they know who's doing it. Or in the case of where I actually live in [this town], there were a number of people who were coming out to my same commute. . . . So I mostly felt. . . . a general sense of recognition. Like, 'Yeah, this is the moment that we live in. People are doing this. It's no big deal.'"

At the same time, some professors did indicate that they had encountered negative reactions from their colleagues as well. Additionally, a few told me that while on the job market, they hid their lifestyle, fearing that search committees might deem them more apt to leave their jobs. "It isn't always acceptable," one respondent who was an academic told me. "There are levels of suspicion." He reconfirmed with me several times that I would conceal his identity for this project.

Joan and J.P.

Joan, a professor in her late forties, and her husband, J.P., who worked outside of academia, had been married for twenty-three years. They had previously lived apart for two years, and were just about to begin another noncohabiting stint when I spoke with them. They now anticipated living apart for the next decade or so, until it was time for retirement. They had no children.

Both Joan and J.P. told me that they had experienced social disapproval for their lifestyle. Joan, for instance, described the reactions of "friends who have taken a much more traditional path": "They're like, 'Well, you know, if it makes you happy. It sounds really crazy and we're pretty sure you're going to be divorced soon' kind of attitude. Because you're not following the traditional path."

J.P. echoed Joan's words when he told me that his family members felt the couple's lifestyle was a pathway to marital dissolution: "Older people, parents, older siblings would sometimes sort of give you the sidelong glance like, 'Eh, they're gonna be divorced pretty soon. They're not living together.' "[4] Like other academic commuters I interviewed, however, J.P. indicated that these negative evaluations of his lifestyle tended to come from outside the academy. He added, "But people in similar situations to ours—grad students and faculty and so on—they totally understood. Because they had gone through it, a lot of them, themselves. Or were in a similar situation. So we didn't get any static at all from our peers."

Also like Dawn and Al, J.P. and Joan indicated that they did not enter into this lifestyle for solely economic reasons. Asked if she had lived apart from J.P. due to financial necessity, Joan explained, "That was part of it, definitely," but she then qualified, "In retrospect, if one of us had been working full time, it could have been a lot more cost-effective, because we certainly spent a good deal of money on plane tickets. And then we had the cost of two households." In response to the same question, J.P. stated more unequivocally: "Um, not so much *financial* necessity. . . . It would have been cheaper to live together, but we were not able to do that" (emphasis in original).

J.P.'s response, framing cohabitation as something that the couple was "not able" to do, coincides with Al's statement that living apart was "just what need[ed] to happen" and with the responses of many other commuters who interpreted living apart within the framework of constraint rather than choice. Yet, while financial concerns were a factor for some respondents (as Joan suggests), Dawn, Al, Joan, and J.P. were typical of the vast majority of my respondents in that they did not view this as the primary factor in their separation. In the sections that follow, drawing on deviance theory, I explore my respondents' narratives about why they entered into these nonnormative arrangements.

"The Decision Was Really Made for Us": Feeling the Strain

I asked my respondents, "Whose decision was it to start living apart?" I included this question based on prior work suggesting that commuter relationships are in part a result of increased female decision-making power within marriage. In response to this question, however, an unexpected discourse emerged. Forty-six respondents—nearly one half (47.4%) of the sample—cited external forces as the reason for their geographic separation rather than interpreting it within the context of either partner's choice.[5] (Most of the others indicated that it was both partners' decision to live apart.) In sum, while the question was framed in terms of active decision-making, these respondents flipped the script, framing their answers in the passive voice and adopting determinist language. One respondent, for instance, gave the name of her husband's boss as the person who had made the decision. Another indicated, "The decision was really made for us." A few used the expression *fait accompli.* Many others persisted in describing the structure and limitations of the couples' two jobs, in response to this question.

Further, while this nonagentic discourse was most salient in responses to the question about decision-making, it appeared at various points throughout these interviews. For example, when asked what advice she might give to spouses who were considering living apart, Vicki, a professor in her mid-forties, replied, "Gosh. Well, I think for me the advice would be more about marriage. It's just: flexibility. You kinda have to go with the flow. Like my friend who said, 'Oh, I would never do that—have a marriage where we lived apart.' Well, life doesn't always work out that way. *We don't always have those options.* And I think making a marriage work is about embracing these changes and learning to work around them and work within them" (emphasis added).

As a group, my interviewees were well educated and they had greater financial resources than other subsets of noncohabiting spouses like undocumented immigrants and blue-collar workers whose jobs involve extensive travel—for instance, commercial fisherman and long-haul truckers (Zvonkovic et al. 2005). Yet, as Vicki's comment illustrates, these relatively privileged couples often felt they had no option but to adopt these atypical lifestyles.

One theoretical framework that is useful for thinking about these non-normative lifestyles is Robert Merton's notion of strain (1938; 1968). Strain theory, at its core, focuses on the connection between broad cultural goals—for instance, financial success—and the structural means for meeting those goals. For Merton, one scenario in which deviance occurs is when individuals who are blocked from attaining cultural goals through legitimate mechanisms attempt to achieve those goals via nonnormative pathways. While Merton's initial work was largely focused on financial barriers to success, recent scholarship has emphasized that strain theory has utility beyond underprivileged groups who participate in deviance due to their lack of access to financial means (e.g., Capowich, Mazerolle, and Piquero 2001; Langton and Piquero 2007; Sharp et al. 2001).[6] For instance, Merton's formulation has been refined by Agnew (2005), who, with his notion of General Strain Theory (GST), has extended it to the avoidance of stressors, or "events or conditions that are disliked by individuals" (4).

My interviewees aspired to (specific) professional careers but were unable to attain such careers within a normative family structure, and so they "innovated"—to use Merton's term (1938, 676). Thus, while "little formal education and few economic resources" (Merton 1938, 679) were not obstructions for these couples, they still encountered barriers. When the requirements of family life created a structural impediment to the achievement of their professional aims, they became innovators, shifting into nonnormative family arrangements in order to attain those goals. Respondents felt these constraints acutely, as illustrated by the prevalence of the nonagentic narratives that emerged spontaneously in response to the question about decision-making.

Is It About the Money, Honey?

What specific strains did commuter spouses feel? As discussed, most respondents said that money was *not* the primary catalyst for their noncohabitation. In fact, when asked, "Would you say that you live[d] apart because of financial necessity?," only twelve respondents (12.4%) replied yes. Further, even those in the "yes" column tended to suggest that "necessity" was an elastic term. Recall Dawn, who replied "yes" but then mused

"What is necessity?" and indicated that the couple "probably" could have "gotten by on one income."

Responses such as Dawn's, however, make sense within the context of contemporary Western capitalism. The commuter spouses in this sample differed from the deviant individuals Merton (1938) originally discussed, who were "asked to orient their conduct toward the prospect of accumulating wealth and . . . largely denied effective opportunities to do so institutionally" (679). My respondents theoretically had access to the institutional mechanisms to attain financial stability (if not, maybe, extreme wealth). Yet, as work on corporate deviance has pointed out, "need" is relative within a capitalist economy that stresses constant accumulation. Nikos Passas (1990), for instance, has made the point that while Merton initially saw the lower classes as more vulnerable to deviance due to their economic position, ". . . as the meaning and content of success goals vary from one part of the social structure to another, similar difficulties in attaining diversely defined goals may be faced by people in the upper social reaches too" (158). Passas viewed this phenomenon as connected with the "ceaseless striving for success" (158) inherent to Western capitalism.[7]

Like Dawn, other commuter spouses embraced relativistic notions of "need" consistent with Passas's argument. For instance, one female respondent exemplified this interpretation of strain theory under capitalism when she drew a distinction between being financially "fine" and "*as* fine":

> *Would you say you're living apart because of financial necessity?*
> Yes and no. Like, we don't—If he quit his job and just found a job here, we'd be fine financially. But because he's so close to retirement, it makes sense to cash out on all that stuff. He gets more if he waits 'til a certain age. . . . If he waits and retires from that company, it will be more beneficial financially.
> *So it's not 'necessary' but it's—[pause] a 'good thing'?*
> Yeah. It's not necessary, but it's probably definitely [*sic*] the reason we're apart, if that makes sense. Like, yeah, he could just quit his job and work here and we'd be fine, but we wouldn't be *as* fine. If that makes sense. (emphasis in original)

At the same time, financial concerns were only one factor in these arrangements, and most respondents indicated that economic need did not drive their noncohabitation. In fact, among the nearly ninety percent of respondents who indicated that they did not live apart due to financial necessity, a nontrivial fraction (18 respondents), like Joan and J.P., explicitly stated that living apart actually cost them money. As Tamra—a respondent in her late twenties who worked in the medical industry—explained, "Uh, no, it's *really* expensive to live apart! We have to pay two rents. It would be so much easier if we could live together and commute but it's not feasible to drive two hours every day" (emphasis in original).

In sum, financial viability is not (for the most part) the cultural goal that dual-income professionals are striving for when they "innovate" via noncohabitating arrangements. For some respondents, money was one driving factor in their lifestyles, although their conceptions of "financial necessity" were relative and specific to a contemporary, Western capitalist context. However, financial strain was not, overall, the *primary* force propelling commuter spouses into these nonnormative arrangements; some even indicated that noncohabitation had a negative financial impact.[8]

It's Not (Only) about the Money, Honey: Professional Strain

Why did a substantial portion of commuter spouses—nearly half—feel that the decision to live apart was out of their hands? As I have discussed, the answer lies partly in their concept of financial need, or relative "need" within a capitalist system of accumulation. However, most respondents said that they did not live apart due to financial necessity. In fact, in response to the question about financial push factors, many commuter spouses drew a clear line between economic concerns and career concerns.

For these respondents, their primary goal in noncohabitation was professional development—a concept that was complexly associated with, but also semidetached from, financial attainment. For example, when asked whose decision it was to start living apart, Pauline immediately answered, "Money." However, when asked if she and her husband lived apart due to financial necessity, she replied, "It's more than that. It's not just financial . . . I mean, we're pretty high income. You know, we could do [*sic*] on his salary. It's career." This distinction between "money" and "career" pervaded many of the responses to this interview question. Recall, for instance, Al's point that they did not live apart due to finances: "But it was more like, this is her professional—this is her career." Ned also explicitly drew this distinction:

> *Would you say that you lived apart because of financial necessity?*
> Ned: You know, I wouldn't. I wouldn't say it was financial necessity. Instead I would call it 'professional necessity.' That we're a two-career couple, and our careers are geography dependent. That we have to go where the jobs are. And so that's why we've had to separate . . . I wouldn't say that money is *not* an issue because money is always an issue, but if it were about money then I could probably get a job that paid me many times more than what I make in the same area, in the same geographic area. So it's not money. It's that we're in professions that necessitate separation. (emphasis in original)

In discussing "professional necessity," Ned gave voice to a concept that many commuter spouses touched upon during their interviews. These responses suggest that one mechanism driving commuter spouses' nonagentic discourse was their extreme investment in their professional role identities. While some, like Ned, acknowledged that they "could probably," theoretically, find jobs geographically close to their partners, these were not their goal jobs.

One useful framework for better understanding this notion of "professional necessity" is Mary Blair-Loy's (2009) concept of devotion. For Blair-Loy, the "schema of work devotion"—which often collides with the "family devotion schema" (though both are ideal-typical)—"defines the career as a calling or vocation that deserves single-minded allegiance and gives meaning and purpose to life" (1–2). In her scholarship on female executives, Blair-Loy traces how the structure of the postindustrial capitalist economy impels professionals to construct such an understanding of their work. For instance, under the 1938 Fair Labor Standards act, salaried workers were not eligible for overtime pay; companies thus began to hire fewer, "elite" workers, who were then expected to work longer hours (2). The work devotion schema, espoused by both employers and employees, helped workers to construct their time away from their families as meaningful. This context is useful for thinking about how commuter marriages come about and are sustained. The meaning of work is part of the impetus for the separation but it also helps to sustain the separation. And ultimately, careers away from their partners, and sometimes children, have become something not just meaningful but crucial—something that "had" to happen.

The concept of professional necessity also resonates with previous social psychological literature on identity and the professions. Other scholarship has attested to the potential durability and salience of professional identity. As Peter Callero (1985) summarizes, "For one person the occupational role-identity may be the dominant aspect of the self, taking precedence over other role-identities and affecting general self-perceptions and actions" (203).[9] Indeed, previous scholarship on commuter spouses has also touched on this theme. Gerstel and Gross (1984), for instance, found that career was the "primary source of personal identity" for the commuters in their sample (35). For many of my interviewees, similarly, their jobs and their specific professional role-identities likely took precedence in the way that they acted and viewed the world.

Somewhat ironically, by going to school and getting advanced degrees in specialized fields—by becoming the "elite" workers Blair-Loy discusses—rather than expanding their employment options, these workers had in a sense reduced their options (as they perceived them). Many respondents discussed the scarcity of jobs fitting their specific training. Joan, for instance, told me that "faculty positions are harder and harder to find. I looked within an eight-hour radius when I was applying for jobs. I had three offers." In fact, in extreme cases, respondents appeared engulfed (Schur 1971) in their professional identities, viewing themselves *only* in specific professional roles to the exclusion of others. When asked, "Did you consider doing something other than living apart?," for example, one respondent who worked in higher education hesitated. "I mean, I don't really understand your question," she said. "I'm a teacher, and there were three job openings in [my field] that year. I applied to all of them and I got this."

In sum, there are intertwined factors at both the macro and micro levels influencing my respondents' assertions that it was "nobody's decision" to live apart. First, increased specialization of the professions on a broader structural level has meant that, for these workers, their relatively high levels of education (and thus relatively long periods of human-capital investment) have effectively limited their potential job prospects as they viewed them, rather than expanding them. This explanation is in line with

Murray-Close's (2013) argument that the elevated prevalence of this lifestyle among those with advanced degrees is likely related to labor market specialization. Secondly, and relatedly, commuter spouses' senses of the meaning of their work—and their highly developed, specific professional identities—may also explain why so many view themselves as without "choice."

"A Better Future": Living Apart and Collectivism

Individualistic concerns such as career advancement and personal fulfillment were not the sole mechanisms behind these arrangements. To extend one of my earlier arguments about the tension between interdependence and autonomy in these relationships, commuters also interpreted their decision to live apart within a framework of collectivism. Asked about their reasons for living apart, some discussed the long-term benefits of noncohabitation, not only for them as individuals but for their marriages and families. These benefits included long-term (if not short-term) financial gain, more stable careers for both partners, and the relocation of one spouse to an area where the whole family ultimately intended to move. One respondent told me, for instance, "It's one year apart, but it'll ultimately make for a better future." Another commuter stated similarly, "If this was a situation where I would have to be in this job for the next five years, I would definitely give it up because I don't want to put work over family. But definitely right now, fifty-two weeks is gonna make our family life stronger. So that's why we chose to do long-distance again." For these spouses, noncohabitation was not just about the opportunity to pursue career-related, individualistic aims; rather, some interpreted the lifestyle as ultimately a boon to the family unit.

The Inertia Narrative

Commuters like the ones above often underscored the brevity of their stints apart, relative to the broader term of their marriages. However, many respondents also told me that they had initially anticipated they would live together for a much shorter time than ended up being the case—an element of the nonagentic discourse I have come to think of as the "inertia narrative." For example, I had the following exchange with one female respondent:

> *When you decided to live apart, whose decision would you say that was?*
> Well, when he took the job, our original thought—because the kids were get-
> ting to the point where they were pretty much out of the house—was that
> we would move up there. But then I was finishing up my [] degree at that
> time and I wasn't sure where I was going to be working, so we thought we
> would just wait a little longer. But he would end up being in a hotel room
> for a couple of nights a week. So then it kind of became clear that it proba-
> bly wasn't practical for us to sell the house and move up there. So the com-
> pany offered to get him an apartment, so he's been in the apartment now
> a couple of nights a week.

Like many interviewees who framed their continued noncohabitation as the outcome of an unexpected sequence of events, rather than a deliberate decision, this commuter emphasized that the seven years they had now spent living apart was longer than they had initially expected. Now, she said, the plan was to live apart for "five to seven" additional years, until her husband's retirement.

Other Narratives of "Choice"

While in this chapter I have explored general patterns in my respondents' discussions of "choice," there was no singular narrative about the decision to begin living apart. For instance, some of my interviewees said that they did live apart from their partners due to financial need. I analyzed the "financial necessity" question conservatively—for instance, coding the response as a "yes" for commuters like Dawn, who said that they lived apart due to financial need but then went on to interpret "need" in a relativistic way. However, a few respondents unequivocally said that they were living apart due to financial need.[10]

Likewise, as discussed, when I asked commuter spouses about their choice to live apart, about half identified forces outside of themselves as being responsible for their noncohabitation, while the other half indicated that both spouses made the decision to live apart. Here, I have focused on those who engaged in a nonagentic discourse. Within the other group—the "choice" group—few elaborated on their responses, although some did in ways that particularly emphasized their own agency. For example, one attorney in her late twenties described living apart as "a calculated move in favor of the jobs that we were pursuing."

Considering the phrasing of the interview question, however, it is striking that more responses were not like hers. Choice was implicit in the question about "whose decision" it was to live apart, yet a substantial portion of interviewees still indicated that neither spouse made this decision. "Do you feel that living apart was a choice?" or a similar question may have yielded even more responses that were focused on structural constraints.

Caveats

There are several caveats to my arguments in this chapter. First, Merton's strain theory has not been immune to critique (for an excellent summary, see Messner and Rosenfeld 1994, 62). To be clear, my analysis here does not imply a total acceptance of this theory, nor an empirical test of this theory. Rather, I identify an unexpected finding: many commuter spouses feel that they have no choice but to enter into these arrangements. And I find that strain theory is a useful theoretical tool for understanding how commuter spouses view their nonnormative lifestyles.

Another caveat is that I collected data during a somewhat unusual time historically: when the United States was in recovery from a financial crisis, following the housing bubble burst of 2007. However, the fact that I conducted the interviews against this economic backdrop in some ways makes these findings even more compelling. One of my primary arguments has been that, while some commuter spouses discussed financial concerns, many felt a sense of exigency about living apart that was not primarily related to money. Perhaps within a rosier economic climate, this finding would have been even more pronounced, with respondents even less likely to discuss financial need as a mechanism behind their noncohabitation.

A third potential objection to my argument here is that my respondents "really do" have choices, in a way that other groups that feel strain—such as Merton's economically strapped deviants—do not. Certainly, as I have emphasized both in this chapter and elsewhere in this book, the commuter spouses in my sample were a relatively privileged group. They were people who should, we would expect, have access to options. Ned, for instance, did not have to find a job in his field or risk financial ruin; as he pointed out, he "could probably" get a position closer to his wife that paid "many times more." Yet he still felt that he and his wife lived apart due to "professional necessity." Whether or not commuter spouses "really" had choices is an interesting philosophical question, but it is not my focus here. The guiding question of this chapter has not been "Do these couples have choices?" but rather "Why do they feel like they do not?" The fact that these respondents are (mostly) white, well-educated professionals in heterosexual marriages and yet they still see themselves as without choice makes this nonagentic narrative all the more interesting.

Interestingly, the way these respondents spoke about their need to live apart resonated with the rhetoric of couples who do live apart for overtly financial reasons. One study of undocumented fruit pickers who migrate from Mexico into the United States, for instance, found that these workers viewed their border crossing and their separations from their families as economically necessary; "There was no other option left for us" was a repeated statement (S. Holmes 2013, 159; see also Castles and Kosack 1973). Primarily white and well educated, and with far greater financial means, the commuter spouses in the present study represented a very different demographic, but they used similarly nonagentic language. At the same time, commuter spouses differed from these other populations in their extreme commitment to their professional identities and their much lower emphasis on economic concerns.

Commuter Spouses and Strain: Broader Implications

To summarize, while focusing on commuter spouses' conceptions of their own agency was not my initial objective with this project, a substantial portion of my respondents engaged in an unexpected and illuminating discourse in response to a question about their decision-making. They described their deviance as exigent—but not necessarily financially exigent. In this chapter, I have demonstrated how we can usefully interpret their nonagentic narrative through the lens of deviance theory. Commuters' experiences with structures and processes at the macro and micro levels—including a capitalist system that influences individual definitions of "choice," highly specialized professional labor markets, and highly developed professional identities—squeeze these couples into atypical arrangements. In addition to illuminating some of the dynamics of commuter marriages, my findings in this chapter have several broader implications.

First, Merton's framework is a useful theoretical tool for understanding these lifestyles, but these findings, in turn, broaden our understanding of the utility of this framework. Unlike the deviant groups Merton discusses, commuter spouses have relatively high levels of education and average or higher incomes. Yet their nonnormative arrangements are formed in response to other structural impediments at the macro level, including limited job opportunities for specialized workers and conventional family structure. Whether or not these couples objectively had "choice" in their arrangements, many felt quite constrained in their decision-making, and it is important to understand why. As sociologists W. I. Thomas and Dorothy Swaine Thomas have noted, "If men define situations as real, they are real in their consequences" (1928, 572). Commuters' perceived lack of options impacted the decisions they made related to their work and their families. In this way, these results extend our understanding of the utility of strain theory and of a deviance frame more generally. While Merton's theory does not fit commuter spouses like a glove, it is a useful tool for conceptualizing how even a relatively privileged population can feel pressured into nonnormative arrangements due to a sense of strain.

Secondly, these findings have repercussions for scholarship on the social psychological implications of work in specialized professional occupations. In particular, they illuminate the concept of "professional necessity"—a not-explicitly-financial nonagentic lens through which many of my interviewees viewed their career moves.

Third, as I discuss further in the book's conclusion, my findings illustrate that commuter spouses, while nonnormative in their living arrangements, highlight a broader incompatibility between the traditional notion of family and the changing structure and meaning of (professional) work. As Steven Messner and Richard Rosenfeld (1994) have argued, also drawing on Merton's work, while Americans tend to extol the concept of "family values," historically policies have devalued the family while overemphasizing the economy (80). To be clear, I am not suggesting that commuter spouses' careers were "more important" to them than their families, per se; if anything, the fact that they wed and remained married in these embattled contexts is perhaps a testament to their allegiance to this normative conception of family. However, these findings do suggest that there is a broader disjuncture between work and family life that becomes particularly salient in this extreme case, where spouses live apart in order to make work/life integration feasible. I return to this point also in the book's conclusion.

Further, commuter spouses are only one type of a larger class of "innovators" who are reshaping the meaning of family in accordance with professional aspirations. Adherence to professional goals may be one reason why women with master's degrees or higher are particularly likely to wait until their thirties to have children or to forego childbearing altogether (G. Livingston 2015). Strain theory is a useful new lens for viewing the structural mismatch between what it means to be a professional worker in a highly specialized labor market and what it means to be a participant in conventional family life. As Gerstel and Gross have pointed out, the model of a small, cohabiting family unit was "outdated" and "outmoded," even in 1984, when they were writing.[11]

In sum, commuter spouses, while atypical in their lifestyle, illuminate several broader tensions between the contemporary structure of work and the conventional structure of family in the United States and are relevant to other types of couples attempting to reconcile their domestic and occupational lives. In the next chapter, I explore how commuters shed light more broadly on the gender dynamics of this work/family disjuncture.

4

"They Don't Have to Pick up Their Husbands' Shoes"

Doing and Undoing Gender

Ethan and Hannah

Ethan was driving through a rainstorm. He was also on the phone with me. Our interview was punctuated by the sound of water pummeling the windows and the constant *swooooosh* of the wipers. We got disconnected twice. Several times, I tried to persuade him to end the interview so that he could concentrate on driving; we could try again later. "It's not worth it—it's only sociology!" The corniness of that line made me sink with embarrassment when I heard it again while transcribing the interview. At the same time, I appreciated Ethan's willingness to speak with me. Like so many of my respondents—who were juggling demanding careers, spouses, children, and the logistics of commuting—he had limitations on his time.

A forty-eight-year-old government employee, Ethan had been living apart from his wife Hannah for the past year of their twenty-one-year marriage. They had two teenaged children who resided with Ethan in the family home, while Hannah lived in an apartment by herself and took a three-and-a-half-hour train ride to see them every weekend. I had spoken with Hannah first. A nonprofit director in her late forties, Hannah was one of the few commuters I interviewed in person. (For further details about interview procedures, see appendix A.) Sitting in her office, where the giant windows offered enviable views of a cityscape, we were wrapping up our talk and beginning to say our goodbyes when Hannah indicated, "I can tell you one thing that [Ethan] is going to say, although I hate to steal his thunder because he loves this line. He will say that I have all of the benefits of a single woman without having to look for a husband, and he has all of the downsides of a divorced man with custody of the children [*laughs*]." When he spoke to me from his rain-pelted car a week later, Ethan did make that statement, unprompted by me, calling it "sort of tongue-in-cheek but also very true."

Indeed, at many points in their interviews, Ethan and Hannah reflected on the gender dynamics of their commuting relationship and how those dynamics intersected (or did not) with normative expectations. Hannah, for instance, discussed how "the front line of childcare" was now her husband, while it had been her prior to her move:

Was that a difficult transition at all?
Hannah: Not for me! [*laughs*]
For him, then?
Hannah: I think he feels the strain, yes. [*laughs*] . . . [I]t's been a lot of work for him. I don't think it's been an unexpected amount of work for him. But the kids are teenagers, too, so it's more driving than childcare. But they're slobs. They make a mess of the house. He's the one who has to clean it up or get on them to clean it up. And he makes them dinner every night. And he's the one who has to drive them places. And he's the one who has to leave work early if somebody's sick or needs a ride somewhere or something like that. Yeah, it's all him.

Ethan, too, underscored the changes in their roles upon Hannah's departure. Asked whether he felt he had taken on more of the childcare responsibilities now, he replied, "That's an understatement, but yes." Further, each spouse suggested that Hannah experienced some prejudice and Ethan experienced praise due in part to the atypical alignment of their genders and roles. As Hannah told me, "[Ethan] supports [this arrangement], but I think he kinda feels like he's doing me a favor. I mean, everyone acknowledges that I'm the one having the fun and he's the one having—making the sacrifices."

> *Who is "everyone" who acknowledges that?*
> Hannah: Well, he and I. And I think the friends. Everyone. It's kind of self-evident to family friends. People realize that he's being a mensch or a saint or whatever.

I asked Hannah if she thought people would consider her a mensch if the gender roles were reversed; "I wonder about that a lot," she replied.

Ethan, too, spoke about social responses to his and his wife's gender roles, predicting that their relationship would be an outlier in my sample: "I'm curious as to how your statistics bear out, but I think it is much more—even in 2012—accepted and expected that the guy is the one who is going off from the homestead and coming back to home on weekends. And much less often the woman. So if I were the one working in [her city] and she were the one back home, I don't think anyone would bat an eye . . . I mean, that's just my impression."

In this chapter I probe these gender differences in commuters' domestic and occupational roles. Drawing on literature about "doing" and "undoing" gender, I explore how narratives related to work/family balance differ between women and men, and how these narratives uphold, or potentially destabilize, conventional gendered processes. Commuter spouses—who ostensibly represent extreme egalitarianism by living apart in service to their dual careers—present a potentially fruitful context in which to investigate atypical gendered performances. And I argue that, in some ways, these nontraditional arrangements were indeed unique sites for the atypical production of gender. For instance, the geographic separation gave some women a kind of "hall pass" from the demands of domestic femininity, increasing their perceived occupational productivity. Still, Ethan was right; normative expectations about gender roles, specifically regarding childcare, also infused these relationships. I conclude the chapter by discussing the implications of these findings, not only for literature on commuters, but also for our understandings of gender, family, and work more broadly.

"They Don't Have to Pick up Their Husbands' Shoes"

Several months into my postdoctoral fellowship at Vanderbilt, a colleague invited me to dinner at his house. I perched on a bar stool at his kitchen island, between his teenage daughter and adorable younger son, snacking on the chips and salsa his wife had laid out prior to the meal. "You should ask Danielle about her book," my colleague urged his daughter. I paused briefly; my last book had been about dominatrices, and I wasn't sure how that conversation would pan out. "She's writing about husbands and wives who live apart from each other." I relaxed a bit. "Who do you think is happier," he asked his kids, "the men or the women?"

Without missing a beat, his daughter replied, "The women are probably happier because they don't have to pick up their husbands' shoes all the time."

Was this bright thirteen-year-old correct? Did commuting arrangements give women a kind of reprieve from domestic duties? Did women, in some ways, fare better in these relationships than their male partners? Another way to frame this question is: how did commuters "do" gender in these relationships, and how did they potentially "undo" it? How did they produce gender in ways that upheld the normative gender structure, and how did they (potentially) destabilize that structure in some ways?

"Doing" and "Undoing" Gender at the Intersection of Home and Work

In asking these questions, I follow in the footsteps of other scholars who have drawn upon the notion of "doing gender" to conceptualize how femininity and masculinity are constructed and reconstructed through microlevel interactions in daily life (e.g., Berk 1985; West and Zimmerman 1987). West and Zimmerman, for instance, focus on the idea of a performer doing a performance within a social context. Delineating between "sex," "sex category," and "gender," these authors describe gender as "the relationship between being a recognizable incumbent of a sex category (which itself takes some doing) and being *accountable* to current cultural conceptions of conduct becoming to—or compatible with the 'essential natures' of—a woman or a man" (2009, 114, emphasis in original). They view gender, then, "as an ongoing situated process, a 'doing' rather than a 'being'" (2009, 114).

At the same time, recent literature has also highlighted the importance of examining contexts in which gender is "undone" (Butler 2004; Deutsch 2007; Risman 2009). Butler (2004) first introduced the latter term, exploring what it might mean "to undo restrictively normative conceptions of sexual and gendered life" (1; see also Pullen and Knights 2007). In this chapter, following scholars such as Connell (1987) and Lorber (1994), I conceptualize gender as a structure, while also attending to the ways in which this structure is sustained through such daily, routinized performances.[1] Furthermore, in the vein of scholars such as Sullivan (2004), I also attend to ways in which daily gendered performances might serve to undermine or change this structure. In exploring both doing and undoing, I investigate commuter marriages as sites in which everyday performances recreate the gender structure, while I also focus on the "potentially transformative" (Sullivan 2004, 209) power of such performances.

Previous scholarship has identified interaction between partners in heterosexual relationships as "among the most significant locations" (Sullivan 2011, 2) for the doing of gender. Dual-income couples must navigate both occupational and domestic gendered roles, as well as the intersection of the two. And these two spheres are, in and of themselves, already gendered. On one hand, as West and Zimmerman have pointed out, "It is not simply that household labor is designated as 'women's work,' but that for a woman to engage in it and a man not to engage in it is to draw on and exhibit the 'essential nature' of each" (1987, 144). On the other hand, the occupational sphere is masculinized and the "ideal" worker a man. As Acker (1990) has observed, within organizational logic, "The closest to the disembodied worker doing the abstract job comes to a real worker is the male worker whose life centers on his full-time, life-long job, while his wife or another woman takes care of his personal needs and his children" (149). In part because of the strongly gendered nature of these spheres, struggles over domestic duties and their interaction with workplace obligations have been central to scholarly conversations about doing and undoing gender.

A primary emphasis of this work/family scholarship has been on the "doing" side—that is, on how performances of gender reproduce the existing gender structure (Sullivan 2004). Indeed, research has emphasized that wives in heterosexual relationships, even when they are employed outside of the home, do more "second shift" (Hochschild 1990) labor than their husbands. That is, women take on a larger share of housework (Berk 1985; Brines 1994; Cleveland, Fisher, and Sawyer 2015), in addition to more caregiving work for children, the elderly, and the disabled (Heymann 2000; National Alliance for Caregiving and AARP 2009). According to the United States Bureau of Labor Statistics, about 56 percent of married mothers who are full-time workers do some housework on an average day, versus only 18 percent of full-time employed, married fathers (2008; based on combined data from 2003–6). Another study, by the Institute for Social Research (Swanbrow 2008) found that, rather than either reducing or increasing housework for both parties, marriage was associated with a reduction in housework for men (one hour per week) but an increase in housework for women (seven hours per week).

Additionally, some research has found that there are gendered dimensions to "spillover" from home to work (Dilworth 2004; Mennino, Rubin, and Brayfield 2005), with women reporting more conflict than men do between work and family roles (Innstrand et al. 2009). These studies suggest that, overall, men are better able than women to separate their paid work and family spheres (Gerson 1985; Thompson and Walker 1989). Finally, the asymmetrical household and childcare contributions of men and women are one factor in the continued "wage penalty" for motherhood (Anderson, Binder, and Krause 2002; Avellar and Smock 2003; Budig and England 2001; Waldfogel 1997), while fathers earn more than childless men (Benard, Paik, and Correll 2007; Lundberg and Rose 2000).

But what about "undoing"? Some more recent research has emphasized that everyday practices within families also potentially undermine or challenge existing relations. There have been long-term, cross-national changes in the gendered division of labor in the domestic sphere (Gershuny 2000; Milkie, Raley, and Bianchi 2012; Sullivan 2004; Sullivan and Gershuny 2001). For instance, in 2000, Suzanne Bianchi, Melissa Milkie, Liana Sayer, and John Robinson pointed out that the amount of time men spent on housework had nearly doubled since 1965. In fact, research suggests that the gaps in the amount of time spent by women and men in both paid work and unpaid domestic labor have narrowed considerably (Sayer 2005) and that this narrowing is due not only to an increase in the domestic contributions of men but also a steep decline in the contributions of women (Bianchi et al. 2000). Dual-income couples, furthermore, are key players in these changes. Men's contributions to childcare are more substantial when their wives are employed (Raley, Bianchi, and Wang 2012).

In sum, while much scholarship surrounding gendered dynamics at the intersection of home and work has focused on doing gender in ways that uphold the normative gender structure, recent work has also highlighted "undoing" by underscoring changes in these everyday practices. Sociologist Barbara Risman (2009) has argued, "As marital norms become more egalitarian, we need to be able to differentiate when husbands and wives are doing gender traditionally and when they are undoing it—or at least trying to undo it" (82). Much prior empirical literature has provided evidence for the former, and some for the latter. In this chapter, I take up Risman's proposition by exploring how commuter marriages might be a potentially fruitful site for transformational gender practices, while also examining how husbands and wives might be "doing gender traditionally," even within these nonnormative arrangements.

Why Would Commuter Spouses Be Different?

Commuter marriages are potentially important contexts in which to analyze atypical gender dynamics, for several reasons. First, as Ethan suggested in his interview, these couples are already undoing gender in a way by not subordinating women's careers to those of their husbands. Both historically and in the present day, marriage has often meant that women set aside their occupational pursuits "for the good of the family" (B. Livingston 2014, 950), and, when faced with work/family conflict, it is wives who have disproportionately done the "scaling back" (Becker and Moen 1999) in their careers. Indeed, gender continues to play a key role in couples' mobility decisions (Clarke, Hyde, and Drennan 2013). Evidence suggests that the majority of couples faced with geographic constraints continue living together (McFall and Murray-Close 2016), and in a majority of cases where "trailing" occurs, it is the woman who trails (Shahnasarian 1991).[2] Women in (heterosexual) commuter marriages either say that they will not follow their husbands, or, in some cases, that they will move for *their* jobs rather than continuing to live with their husbands.

(See my discussion about these two pathways in appendix A). Commuter spouses, who make nonnormative career decisions, potentially illuminate how gender may remade in other ways.

Commuter marriages also present a key site at which to investigate gender's undoing because of the geographic separation of domestic and occupational spheres. As discussed, some prior research suggests that women experience more conflict than men do between paid work and family spheres. However, we might expect the commuting lifestyle to present an ideal context for role segmentation. In particular, previous scholarship suggests that treating home and work as separate physical spaces is effective in reducing spillover; this physical separation enables individuals to stake out distinct "territories of the self" related to each realm (Nippert-Eng 1996, 569). We might expect that women are uniquely able to undo their work/family entanglements in commuting relationships.

Based on this prior scholarship, I pose the following question: in what ways might gender be undone by women and men in commuter marriages, and in what ways is it done—specifically as relates to work/family balance? Following Risman's exhortation to seek out spaces in which husbands and wives are undoing (or attempting to undo) gender, I begin from the premise that commuter spouses, with their emphasis on wives' careers and geographic detachment of family and work, represent a potentially illuminating context in which to analyze such undoing. At the same time, these relationships are also useful for further clarifying how gender might be done in traditional ways that uphold the conventional gender structure, even in seemingly egalitarian, nonnormative relationships.

In the sections that follow, I first focus on how undoing occurs in these relationships. I then turn to mechanisms through which commuters' gendered performances at the intersection of home and work reproduce the conventional gender structure.

Lily and Mark: The "Undoing"

Lily was a professor in her late fifties. She and her husband Mark had been married for three decades and had lived apart at several points during that time—most recently, on opposite coasts of the United States. While they were apart, Mark had typically flown to visit Lily at least every other weekend. She flew back to see him during academic holidays. At the time of both of their interviews, however, they had again resumed cohabitation. They had no children.

When asked whether there was anything she had liked about living apart from her husband, Lily replied, "Well, I got my work done. That's for damn sure. If you have no distractions whatsoever, you certainly do get to do the work. I worked and got tenured and did a few other things in terms of professionally."

By contrast, her husband Mark—a respondent in his mid-fifties who worked in the finance industry—had a different narrative about his gains from noncohabitation. An enthusiastic and garrulous interviewee, Mark spoke more effusively than most respondents about the benefits of a commuter lifestyle. When asked what, if anything, he had liked about living apart from Lily, he gave multiple responses. For instance, he explained that noncohabitation had in some ways made the relationship more enjoyable ("It was like we were perpetually dating") and had contributed to the overall quality of their marriage. Yet, unlike his wife, he did not touch upon increased occupational productivity as a theme.

Lily's and Mark's narratives, like those of many respondents, suggested that commuting arrangements could enable role segmentation, reducing some types of work/family conflict; however, this finding was highly gendered.

Work/Family Conflict, for Women and Men: The "Undoing"

While male commuters did speak about how living apart had increased their productivity at work, this narrative was far more pronounced among female respondents, who also engaged in distinctly gendered narratives about that productivity. Isha explained, for instance, "I was able to do a lot intellectually. In a strange way, my time was my own. . . . Most of the time I was working. I did a lot of work, very late up at night. . . . So that was good because I don't think I could have actually achieved what I was able to achieve [if we had been living together]." By framing her productivity as unusual ("in a strange way"), Isha suggested that this represented a deviation from her standard experience. Replies like Lily's and Isha's suggested that for some women in commuter relationships, not only typical practices surrounding work and home were being undone but also gender itself.

These differences between men's and women's narratives about productivity can be usefully contextualized within previous literature on the gendered dimensions of work/family conflict. As discussed, some research (Dilworth 2004; Gerson 1985; Innstrand et al. 2009; Mennino, Rubin, and Brayfield 2005; Thompson and Walker 1989) has indicated that women encounter more "spillover" between home and work and generally have more difficulty than men in segmenting the two spheres. The narratives of commuter spouses suggest that, when the two spheres are separated geographically, women more profoundly experience the advantage of being able to concentrate on only one sphere.

Noncohabitation and Household Obligations: The "Undoing"

Different role expectations for men and women surrounding household work factored into this gender difference in the impact of noncohabitation on productivity. Women tended to report a diminution in their household labor when living apart, whereas for many men it was the opposite. For instance, when asked what he liked least about living apart, one male respondent—a corporate executive in his mid-fifties—replied, "As someone who never cooked, or cooked very rarely, I would say one of the biggest adjustments of living apart is figuring out how to do the stuff that your spouse has done for you for the most part for your entire adult life."

On the contrary, women interviewees commonly discussed their decreases in household labor. For instance, Jeana, an attorney in her late thirties, had recently resumed cohabitating with her husband, from whom she had been living apart while he participated in a medical residency a three-hour drive from their shared home. They had no children. Jeana told me, "I think to some extent there were components that I really did like about living alone again. You know, [my husband] and I will laugh about this, but it *was* nice to have my own space and to not have to clean up after his crap all the time" (emphasis in original).

Responses like Jeana's suggest that my colleague's daughter may have been prescient in her remarks about wives picking up their husbands' shoes. They also resonate with the Institute for Social Research report suggesting that entering into (cohabitating) marriage increases women's housework but decreases men's (Swanbrow 2008), as well as the broader body of scholarship on the persistent asymmetrical gendered division of domestic labor, despite the fact that men are doing more housework than they have done in the past (e.g., Bianchi et al. 2000). By reallocating the division of labor, noncohabitation brings the asymmetrical nature of that division into sharp focus. This reallocation constitutes a kind of "undoing" as both men and women commuters—oppositely—experience transformations in how they engage with everyday household work.

Gender Salience in Women's Narratives: The "Undoing"

Moreover, some women respondents, but no men respondents, explicitly referenced gender in their accounts of their increased productivity. These women's responses suggested they were thoughtful about the connection between their role expectations as women, their noncohabitation, and their professional goals.

For example, Sonja was a professor in her late thirties who had been living apart from her husband a few days a week for about eleven years. The couple had a five-year-old daughter who resided with Sonja's husband in the family home (an atypical scenario, as I discuss in the following section). Late in our interview, Sonja and I had the following exchange:

> *So, what if anything would you say that you like the least about living apart from your husband?*
> Sonja: Um [*long pause*] it's funny because I just thought of more things I like about it [*laughs*].
> [*laughs*] *So, maybe you could answer that first!*
> Sonja: Okay [*laughs*]. I like the ability to focus. To turn off all family, community and just focus on work. Work three days straight. Immerse myself. . . . The ability to immerse without distraction, without competing obligations. It's important to me. It enables me to be a passionate worker and to really connect with my job and to put 110 percent into

the job. So, yeah. That's one thing I really love about the apart-together thing. I think that for the individuals I know who are married, living in the same household, the woman's job oftentimes gets subsumed or ignored or marginalized in the day to day. And there are a number of reasons for that—I'm sure we can all figure out. But I think this helps me to have a separate—to protect that part of my life: my career, my passion for what I do.

Sonja's comment that noncohabitation allowed her to "protect" her career by "turning off" her family obligations is not only consistent with the narratives of many women commuters, but it also resonates with prior research indicating that productivity is facilitated when workers can construct home and career as distinct "territories of the self" (Nippert-Eng 1996).

Like Sonja and many other female respondents, Hannah also discussed being able to carve out time to work while she was away from the family home. "Part of the reason that this is possible and part of the reason that I'm able to work at home on Fridays is that when I'm here Monday through Thursday, I just work," she told me. "You know, I just stay. And I've never had that luxury before because my work life is always the one that's been circumscribed by the needs of the kids. If somebody has to leave school early, then I would leave work early. I don't have that here. So I just work."

Hannah's assertion that her ability to engage in work without restriction was unusual ("I've never had that luxury before") further reveals how role segmentation can be directly linked to the subversion of normative gendered expectations, as discussed above. Many women, like Sonja and Hannah, felt that one benefit of this lifestyle was that it relieved some sources of strain related to gendered expectations at the intersection of work and home. These women suggested that they were able to undo gender through engagement in nonnormative behaviors—like pulling all-nighters or pouring "110 percent" into their careers—and the geographic separation allowed them to create the physical and mental space in which to do this. In a sense, they were able to approximate Acker's (1990) masculinized, "disembodied worker" (149) who, unburdened by familial and other domestic obligations, exists only for the work.

"I Was Single-Parenting Again": The "Doing"

While it was often difficult to schedule interviews with commuter spouses given their hectic work and travel schedules, it was particularly challenging to find a time to speak with Elise. Elise (an academic in her late twenties) and her husband Peter (a business owner) had a one-year-old son together and saw each other irregularly; at some points they would be together for a month or more, while at other times they would see each other only about two or three times a month. At the beginning of our interview, Elise apologized for the delay and for a prior cancellation, noting that her husband had been gone and she "was single-parenting again."

Many commuter spouses like Elise, who were the primary caretakers of children, referred to themselves as "single parents" during their interviews. It is important to note that this was not terminology that I used but rather it emanated from respondents. The concept of "single parenting" became part of a discourse about the particular challenges of juggling children and careers within these commuting arrangements. For example, Luann—who was now back to cohabitating with her husband and their nine-year-old and seven-year-old—used the term to describe herself during the time that she and her spouse had lived apart:

> *It's interesting that you described yourself as a "single parent." Is that how you felt?*
> Luann: I definitely felt like a single parent. I mean, I had all of the problems of a single parent with no support system. Literally when I moved [here] . . . I was all on my own except for if I could—a couple of times my mother came to stay with me to help out. But like when I enrolled the children in school they make you fill out these forms, like 'who to contact in case of an emergency.' And I put down my mother's name and phone number. And they were like, 'We have to have somebody who's local.' And I was like, 'Well, I don't have anybody I can write down.'

Later in the interview, Luann emphasized that it was her work schedule that would be interrupted when her children fell ill or had other needs. "When the kids were living with me and I was single-parenting, I took on all of these duties. Like, I *was* a single parent, essentially, for ten months out of the year" (emphasis in original). Respondents like Luann stood in stark contrast to the women discussed in the prior section. Although there were some outliers—as in the case of Isha, quoted above, who had teenage children when she lived apart from her spouse—primary caregivers of minor children did not, for the most part, interpret living apart as a boon to their job productivity. Moreover, these primary caregivers were overwhelmingly women.

These findings not only bolster some previous research suggesting that cultural expectations surrounding women and caregiving behavior continue to persist in long-distance relationships (Bergen, Kirby, and McBride 2007; M. Holmes 2004a) but also add a dimension to scholarship on the relationship between gender, work, and childcare roles.[3] In the sense that mothers were much more likely than fathers to be the primary caretakers of children, commuter spouses "did" their gender in a way that upheld the conventional order. But it was not only that mothers in these relationships were doing more, or most, of the childcare-related "second shift" (Hochschild 1990) work in these relationships. It was even more than that. Many of these women felt that, during periods of noncohabitation, they were doing *all* of it. That is, the relationship between caregiving and femininity was not only replicated but, in some senses, exacerbated in these nonnormative, seemingly egalitarian arrangements.

Finally, there was some evidence that commuter wives were disproportionately responsible for other forms of caretaking beyond child-rearing. A few women respondents discussed the demands of elder care, for instance. However, these particular findings should be interpreted cautiously due to the small number of cases.

Furry Children: Caring for Pets

Caring for pets was another type of domestic work in which commuters engaged. While I had no questions on the interview schedule about this topic, respondents discussed their dogs and cats so frequently that I ended up giving "pets" their own code in my qualitative analysis. One place in which respondents commonly mentioned pets was when I asked if they had any children. There, interviewees both with and without children underscored the difficulties of coordinating pet care in a commuting relationship. For instance, I had the following exchange with one male respondent:

Do you have any children?
No.

Okay. And do you—
—Whoa whoa whoa. We do have two dogs that we treat like children. And are a powerful part of our lives. And come into play. She keeps the dogs when I go away for work, and I miss them terribly when I'm away from them. So it's part of the pain of the separation.

Women more often than men talked about doing care and maintenance of pets while, as in the case of the above respondent, men were more likely to discuss the emotional aspects of their separation from pets. When I asked what, if anything, he liked the least about living apart, for instance, a different male interviewee explained:

Two things, and I gotta be careful the order I put these in. Number one is definitely not seeing [my wife]. And number two . . . I miss seeing the dog during the week. We now have a three-year-old golden retriever. It's a distant second, but not going home every night and opening the garage door and seeing [my wife] and the dog and the dog's tail is going back and forth like she's never seen me before. So I think those are the two things I miss the most. First and foremost, [my wife]. But I'll tell you, if I've had a stressful day, I'll talk to [my wife] but what I'll also do is I'll sit on the living room floor and the dog comes over, sits in my lap. For me, if you wanna talk about a stress-reliever—she's sitting there and I'm petting her, and it's a stress-reliever.

This gender dynamic surrounding pet care made logistical sense, since women were more often the ones continuing to reside in formerly shared family homes, while men more often lived in "satellite" residences. Still, it is important to note that this element of domestic work, too, was gendered—with women more often than their partners falling into these caregiving roles.

Domestic Labor: Outsourcing, Sidestepping, "Doing," and "Undoing"?

Finally, it is important to discuss the household work that these commuters did not do. The concept of outsourcing was a major theme in these relatively privileged respondents' discussions of household labor. Both women and men commuters—but more often men—told me that they outsourced their cleaning and cooking during their periods of noncohabitation.

Asked how she and her husband divided up cooking and cleaning, for instance, one female commuter replied that, while they were apart, "[My husband] ate frozen meals and drive-through [food]. So I did everything." However, she later added, "Of course we have a maid." Similarly, another female respondent said that while she and her husband had shared household tasks when they lived together, "Since we've lived apart, I've definitely carried, like—[he] would agree—about ninety, ninety five percent of the physical work in our shared home. And he does not really take the responsibility in his home by himself. Like he hired someone to come clean and someone to do his laundry for him."

Some interviewees also emphasized that they outsourced their housework even during periods of cohabitation, precisely to sidestep tensions around the very sort of gendered dynamics that I discuss in this chapter. For instance, a female commuter indicated that, early in her relationship with her husband, she had felt resentment about taking on the lion's share of the cleaning: "Now we just farm it out, which has been awesome. Not only do we not have to do it, but there's not disagreements about it." In fact, some respondents told me that the commuting arrangement itself had helped to dissipate some of this tension. One respondent, for example, shared that she found it easier to deal with her husband's messiness now that they lived in separate houses: "I think when you think of yourself as a guest you're kinder and more polite and more accepting. And if I wasn't in that mode, I think I would be bitchier and angrier."

On one hand, it might be tempting to interpret this outsourcing, for women, solely as "undoing" gender, since it enables them to bypass some participation in stereotypical "women's work." On the other hand, the fact that husbands more often than wives relied on these outsourced forms of labor aligns with normative role expectations surrounding gender and household work.

Moreover, as sociologists Irene Browne and Joya Misra have pointed out (2003), the organization of paid domestic labor itself reproduces the gender structure as well as other forms of social stratification. "Domestic work is deeply imbedded in hierarchies of class, gender, race, ethnicity, and nationality," they explain. "Not only are domestic tasks associated with one gender (women), but gendered norms of childcare and housework being seen as 'natural' for women devalue domestic work and workers" (502). While I did not ask commuter spouses about the demographics of the people whom they had hired to do their housework, historically this type of labor has been performed by low-income women from racial and ethnic minority groups (Browne and Misra 2003). In sum, the outsourcing of household work in the commuter marriage is symptomatic not of a radical realignment of gender and work but rather a "work transfer system" (Parreñas 2001, 78) of labor from one group of women to another. Women, whether commuters or their employees, were likely still doing more of the cleaning—and still "doing gender"—in these arrangements.

Outliers

Ethan was right when he suggested that he and Hannah might be outliers. As discussed, in the vast majority of commuter families with children, those kids lived with their mothers full time.[4] However, across all of the couples involved in this study—which includes cases in which I did not interview the other spouse—there were three instances in which minor children resided with their fathers. One thing these three scenarios had in common was that, in each of these instances, the woman was the one who had moved to a "satellite" residence, while her husband remained in the shared family home. This may suggest that the association between femininity and childcare did not override a desire to keep children rooted. However, there were also some instances in which women had moved and brought their children with them—for example, as in the case of Luann, described above.[5]

One of the striking things about outliers when it came to gender and domestic roles was that they tended to know they were outliers and to discuss this fact without prompting. Indeed, unusual couples like Ethan and Hannah were "the exceptions that prove the rule," shedding light on broader, normative dynamics through their cognizance of their atypical roles.

A Caveat

At the beginning of this chapter, I argued that commuter marriages—in which husbands' and wives' careers are, ostensibly, both valued and wives do not "trail"—are potentially fruitful contexts for the enactment of nontraditional gender roles. However, commuter spouses have also selected into marriage—an institution through which gender norms have historically been duplicated (B. Livingston 2014). So, while these relationships are a prime site for "undoing" gender, they are not, potentially, the most apt. Perhaps for a more extreme example, we might look to a group such as the unmarried LATs (couples living apart together) in Levin's (2004) sample. However, previous research suggests that norms surrounding masculinity and femininity are durable, even in such nontraditional arrangements (Lyssens-Danneboom and Mortelmans 2014).

Gender as a Stuck Zipper: Conclusions

In this chapter, I have asked how participants in commuter marriages "do" their gender at the intersection of home and work, and also how they might "undo" it. In fact, commuter marriages are at once contexts where people can perform gender nonnormatively and testaments to the durability of gender and familial norms in nontraditional spaces. Gender, in these relationships, is a bit like a stuck zipper—somewhat undone, but never fully.

This stickiness is highlighted when I compare my findings with older scholarship on commuter marriages. On one hand, some of this prior research may seem antiquated today. Gerstel and Gross (1984), for instance, argued that "women, limited to a marginal position in the labor force, identify themselves (and are seen by others) as their husbands' wives rather than as unique individuals" (18, drawing on Papanek 1973). In more recent years, women have certainly become less "marginal" to the U.S. workforce. According to a 2013 report from the Pew Research Center, for instance, women made up almost of half (47%) of the U.S. labor force, with the employment rate of married mothers with children increasing from 37 percent in 1968 to 65 percent in 2011. Moreover, 40 percent of all households with children under the age of 18 include mothers who are either the sole or primary source of income for the family (Wang, Parker, and Taylor 2013).

On the other hand, despite these major social shifts in the more than three decades since Gerstel and Gross wrote about commuter spouses, my findings bear striking similarities to theirs in some respects. For many female commuter spouses, Gerstel and Gross observed, "Living alone does not introduce the sense of disorder or strain that characterizes so many of their commuter husbands. Quite the reverse—without interruptions and conflicting obligations, commuter wives enjoy greater involvement in professional lives" (118). This parallel between their findings and mine further exemplifies the stickiness of dynamics surrounding gender in these relationships even as, in other respects, society has marched on.[6]

In addition to intersecting with prior empirical research on commuter spouses, my findings in this chapter also support and extend broader scholarship on gender, work, and family in several key ways. First, they add another layer to research suggesting that it is important to seek out sites of "undoing," rather than solely calling attention to how gendered practices surrounding home and work systematically reproduce the gender structure. The commuting arrangement facilitates role segmentation for some women, enabling them to detach home and work and become hyperproductive, stereotypically "masculine" workers. By highlighting the atypical production of gender within this arrangement, this chapter enriches literature suggesting that there are contexts in which norms surrounding gender, work, and family are being reshaped in some ways.

At the same time, these findings also contribute to research suggesting that gendered practices surrounding home and work—even within nonnormative, seemingly egalitarian arrangements—continue to sustain the conventional gender structure. In commuter marriages, some women enact "masculinized" labor practices and some men enact "feminized" home practices, but these relationships also reflect the durability of gender norms. To return to West and Zimmerman's formulation of "doing gender," husbands and wives in these marriages are still beholden to the expectations for their "sex category" (2009, 114) when it comes to the navigation of work and home, and they continue to meet these expectations in some ways. This point about the inescapability of gender norms resonates with previous scholarship on commuter spouses. For instance, research has suggested that commuter wives—who, as discussed in the previous chapter, are more likely than their husbands to experience stigmatization for their lifestyle—are called on to justify their relationships to others who interpret them within normative, hegemonic frameworks (Bergen 2010a; Bergen, Kirby, and McBride 2007; McBride and Bergen 2014).

More broadly, my findings align with prior research about the asymmetrical division of household labor among dual-earning couples. They suggest that, while commuter couples are pioneers in some ways, they also exhibit gendered dynamics that have been associated with broader social disparities, such as the motherhood penalty, among spouses who live together. Here I have focused on dynamics related to the synthesis of work and family roles. In the next chapter, I extend this discussion by probing other types of differences in the lived experiences of women and men in these relationships.

5

WHO BENEFITS FROM
(COMMUTER) MARRIAGE?

Jeff and Bethany

Jeff was explaining how much he loves his job. A fifty-four-year-old vice president of a company (unnamed to preserve anonymity), he had been living apart from his wife Bethany for eight years when I interviewed him by phone in the summer of 2013. The couple had several grown children as well as a young grandson who lived close to Bethany. Jeff, who did all of the traveling, worked in an office a three-hour flight away from the family home. They planned to continue in the current arrangement until his retirement, which would not be for at least another decade.

Although he indicated that he and his wife would prefer to live together, in general Jeff was quite positive about their experience of being in a commuter marriage. "I've been blessed to have a good income all of our life," he explained. "Our kids' colleges are pretty much paid off, my house is paid off, [and] we have a home on the beach. So I could retire if I wanted to. But . . . I enjoy what I'm doing."

Bethany, too, had positive things to say about their commuting relationship, though she focused more on the theme of individual freedom, rather than the financial benefits of the arrangement. When I asked her what, if anything, she liked the most about living apart, she laughed. "What do I like the most?" she responded. "Well I can pretty much do whatever I want [*laughs*]. And I do anyway, when he's here or not here it doesn't really matter. But, like, if I want to go to lunch with a friend, I go out to lunch with a friend. If I want to go out to a movie, I do that. If I wanna sit on the couch and watch TV, I can do that. I don't feel like [I'm] not contributing or something like that."

At another point in the interview, I asked her whether she thought anyone was envious of, or admired, her commuter marriage. She replied, "Yeah, I think people do kind of [envy this lifestyle]—unless you have little kids. When you have little ones I don't think people would admire it, but when your kids are grown, I think people say, 'Oh, I think that's a pretty good deal. I wish my husband traveled!' [*laughs*] So it's good for relationships."

> **Is* it good for relationships, do you think?*
> Bethany: I think if you have a good relationship it is. Like, it works really well for us.

While Jeff agreed that the lifestyle worked well for the couple, when I asked him the same question about whether anyone admired his relationship, he responded in the negative: "I think most people looking in think it's kind of crazy or it's hard."

Bethany and Jeff—both content in their professedly nonideal relationship—talked about their relationship in ways that mirrored broader gendered trends across the commuters in my sample. In the previous chapter, I discussed how women seemed to "do better" than men, in some contexts and in some ways, in these relationships. Specifically, noncohabitation seemed to give some wives a kind of "hall pass" from some of the demands of domestic femininity (while intensifying other demands, such as childcare) as well as providing them with mental and physical space. In this chapter, continuing on the theme of gendered experiences in commuter relationships, I focus on what men and women may gain and lose within these arrangements.

Below, I focus on scholarship indicating that, historically, marriage has benefitted husbands more than wives in some key ways. However, more recent research has suggested that these gender differences may not be as pronounced as they once were—or, perhaps, that they have become nonexistent. I argue that, from the perspective of this literature, commuter spouses are a particularly illuminating population. These couples have access to many of the potential benefits of marriage (such as financial pooling) but, after having spent time both apart and together, they are uniquely reflective about what they gain and lose from the cohabitation aspect of their relationships.

I then trace three types of themes that arose in my interviews with commuter spouses: additional leisure time as a positive aspect of living apart, the importance of social connections (or lack thereof) outside of the immediate commuter family, and outsiders' envy of these relationships. All of these narrative threads are relevant to the benefits or drawbacks of these commuting relationships, and all of them highlight key ways in which husbands and wives tended to perceive and experience these relationships differently. I conclude by arguing that what these spouses "get" or "lose" from living apart is strongly gendered. These differences reflect broader gender dynamics while also demonstrating how commuters are reconfiguring marital roles in important ways.

Who Benefits? Women, Men, and Marriage

A couple of things happened last week. First, my mother sent me a clipping from a news story indicating that divorced women were less likely to want to remarry than their male exes.[1] *"For your research," she had written helpfully with a sharpie in the corner. She had also drawn a heart.*

Next, I was at the dentist. He and his staff had seen a profile of my work on commuter marriage in a local newspaper, and he said they had been anxious to speak with me about it. He waited until my mouth was filled with a saliva ejector and cotton to ask me to elaborate on my findings. I gurgled a response. He removed the cotton.

"Well," I said, "in some ways the women seem happier than the men."

"Of course!" said the hygienist, with a chuckle.

He looked at her. "Really?"

"Oh, yeah. You get to be married but you don't have to deal with your husband all the time?" She stuck the gauze back in my mouth.

"I guess that's true," the dentist said after a little while, and proceeded to tell me about how several of his friends had gotten divorced as soon as their children had left the nest. The men were already looking for new partners, he said, while their ex-wives did not appear to have similar aims.

"Makes complete sense," said the hygienist. "Keep breathing through your nose, honey."

Despite enduring cultural stereotypes about ebullient, raucous bachelorhood and melancholy spinsterhood (Bradburn 1969), research has long found that men actually receive some disproportionate benefits from marriage. Going back to the late 1800s, sociologist Emile Durkheim ([1897] 1951) demonstrated that marriage had a preservative effect against suicide that only benefitted men. In fact, he found the highest rates of suicide to be among divorced men and married women. Throughout at least the next century, researchers produced work that was in line with Durkheim's findings (e.g., Cashion 1970; Gove 1973; Lynch 1977; Radloff 1975). As Robert Coombs summarized in a 1991 literature review, "Marriage is particularly rewarding for men" and "the evidence is consistent with the protection/support hypothesis that a marital partner who provides companionship and psychic aid buffers individuals against physical and emotional pathology" (97). In sum, scholars have attributed men's disproportionate physical and mental health benefits from marriage (Gove 1973), at least in part, to the disproportionate supportive, emotional labor performed by wives.

Yet more recent research has suggested that these male gains from marriage are now diminishing—or have perhaps even become nonexistent. In a 2003 article provocatively titled "Has the Future of Marriage Arrived?," for instance, sociologist Kristi Williams found that "with few exceptions, the effects of marital status, marital transitions, and marital quality on psychological well-being are similar for men and women" (470). Other research from the late 1990s and early to mid-2000s has drawn similar conclusions. For example, a 1998 study looking across seventeen nations found that marriage increased happiness equally among husbands and wives (Stack and Eshleman; see also Simon 2002). These studies suggest that changing gender roles in marriage—and changing gender roles more broadly—have tempered some of the benefits historically felt disproportionately by husbands.

Still, some recent studies continue to indicate differences in the benefits that men and women reap from marriage. For instance, some research conducted as late as 2000 has suggested that, while the "gender gap in happiness" has narrowed, men married to women still find the most happiness within the institution of marriage (Amato et al. 2003, 11). Further, men still appear to be more reliant on the emotional support of their spouses than vice versa (B. Livingston 2014). At the same time, women have historically, and still do, benefit disproportionately from heterosexual marriage in an economic sense. Indeed, one 2004 study found that women gain roughly 55 percent in needs-adjusted, total family income, regardless of whether they cohabit or marry, while men's needs-adjusted income levels remain unchanged upon cohabitation or marriage (Light 2004, 263). Women also gain greater financial benefits from heterosexual remarriage than do men (Ozawa and Yoon 2002).

Commuter spouses are people who choose to get married and who are able to reap the potential financial benefits from that union. Indeed, while I did not specifically ask my respondents if they shared bank accounts with their spouses, many spontaneously mentioned that they did, while others referred to their collective income as "ours." Further, as discussed in chapter 1, financial reliance was one salient subtheme within their discourse of interdependence. At the same time, commuters are a particularly interesting population to examine through the lens of this prior literature because of how they are not like cohabiting spouses. They move through periods of apartness and togetherness, and so we might expect them to be uniquely attuned into the ways in which cohabitation impacts their daily experiences, both positively and negatively.

Who Benefits? Women, Men, and Commuter Marriage

While previous literature on long-distance relationships has found that women tend to have a disproportionate burden in some senses (e.g., childcare), it also suggests that women may disproportionately benefit from these relationships in some key ways. In their 1984 book on commuter spouses, for instance, Gerstel and Gross found that their respondents welcomed the fact that there were "fewer demands and fewer constraints" on their time in the absence of their partners. They continued, "Interestingly, men and women do not value this simplification equally. Though a few men make such comments, almost all the women do, and it is women who celebrate the attendant joys" (116).

Of course, as explored in the previous chapter, gendered experiences of heterosexual relationships have shifted somewhat since 1984. Yet recent literature suggests that, despite these shifts, women still benefit uniquely from long-distance arrangements today. Writing about LAT couples, for instance, Levin (2004) has observed that "few men, but many women" view these arrangements as advantageous, and that women are more often the ones suggesting that the couple live apart (238). Levin gave the example of one woman who preferred being in this arrangement because "she enjoyed the freedom of only being responsible for herself. . . . She simply did what she wanted to do whenever she wanted to do so, and she enjoyed the realization that no one expected her to 'boil the potatoes' each and every day" (234).

Mind the Leisure Gap: Commuters, Gender, and Free Time

Levin's example, and Gerstel and Gross's finding, tie into my discussion in the prior chapter about women's disproportionate domestic work, as well as aligning with a broader literature about the gender gap in recreational time. In the first decade of the twenty-first century, scholars began pointing to a "leisure gap" between men and women where none had existed before. In one 2003 study, for instance, Marybeth Mattingly and Suzanne Bianchi found that men tended to have more "free time" than women, and that marriage and parenthood appeared to widen this gap (999). Research has also found women's free time to be of lower quality than men's; for instance, women's leisure time is more likely to be interrupted, particularly by the demands of unpaid work (Bittman and Wacjman 2000).

It is perhaps because of this gap that female commuters seem to experience a more profound increase in personal leisure time—in "me time," to use the colloquialism—when they enter into these arrangements. Much like Gerstel and Gross, I found that, while only a few male respondents said that these arrangements gave them more time for themselves, most women discussed this benefit. This narrative most often emerged in response to the questions, "What, if anything, do you like *most* about living apart from your spouse?" and "Are there people who envy or admire your arrangement?" For instance, when asked the latter question, Lydia replied, "Just before talking to you today, actually, I was talking to someone who was saying there's—there can be something sort of nice about having the kind of relationship where you have, maybe two nights apart or something like that. Because it lets you take the selfish things that you wanna do, like watch a junk TV show or something, when you're not together, and not feel guilty about—that you're not spending time with your spouse." Lydia told me that she agreed wholeheartedly with her friend.

In the previous chapter, I discussed how commuting arrangements in some senses crystallized traditionally gendered caretaking roles. However, while the "me time" narrative was especially prominent among female commuters without children, those who were the primary caregivers of minors participated in this narrative as well. For instance, Erika, a thirty-two-year-old mother of three who had been living apart from her husband for about two years when I interviewed her, explicitly described this alone time as meaningful because she had children, "Physically, the burden is harder, but, on a day-to-day night, like, I fall asleep faster without [my husband] here. I feel I do get, like, a little more—a break in the evening, because it's not like I have to, um, I know it sounds mean, but like talk to him or engage with him, or, 'Let's watch a TV show together,' or some—or, you know, something like that. It's just like, my alone time. And as a mom, it's so rare to have 'alone-alone' time."

Erika, like many people I interviewed, said that there were many negative things about living apart—for instance, the increased burden of solo childcare. Yet she also echoed the words of other female commuters who focused on the respite these arrangements offered from domestic, emotional, and interactive labor. In sum, more than men, women commuters emphasized that these relationships provided autonomy. Living apart also provided the ability to perform leisure activities independently and—to return to the concept of "mental space" introduced in chapter 2—to carve out mental and emotional "personal" time.

This notion of "me time" connects with other literature suggesting that while men and women both must perform mental and emotional labor in relationships, the dimensions of that work are gendered. Sociologist Lisa Wade (2017), discussing the gender gap in marital happiness, has observed that "women's minds are busy, distracted by the essential work of attending to the needs of others and, because of this, they can feel like their minds are not truly their own." After she wrote a piece for *Money. com* about women's "invisible workload" (2016), Wade found that "in comments across the internet, women responded to my conclusion that women are denied a 'lightness of mind' with a resounding 'yes!' 'amen!' 'thank you!' and 'exactly!' " While commuter marriages may not benefit women in some ways, these relationships can also provide women with the "alone-alone" time (to quote Erika) that is generally more elusive for them than for their male counterparts. For some female commuters, living apart meant having not only more time to perform leisure activities but also more time to privilege their own mental needs.

Doesn't Mean I'm Lonely When I'm Alone: Gender, Loneliness, and Social Ties

In addition to more often describing noncohabitation as a boon to their leisure time, female commuters were also much more likely than men to emphasize the importance of social ties outside of their nuclear families. In their interviews, two thirds of female respondents (66.7%; n=40) discussed how friends, colleagues, and/or extended family played a positive role in their lives during periods of noncohabitation—compared to only about one fifth (21.6%; n=8) of men.

For instance, an academic who had lived apart from her husband for six years while he worked overseas, told me that, although the arrangement was at times quite difficult for herself and her children, "I had really, really good friends." In fact, when I asked what, if anything, she liked most about living apart from her husband she again asserted, "I made some really, really good women friends. Women who were older, or single, or divorced, or just here or whatever. We were really close. I had a really good community of women."

Bethany, whom I profiled at the beginning of this chapter, similarly discussed the positive role of her social network while Jeff was away. "I don't really get lonely," she explained, "because my kids are here and I'm seeing them or going to lunch or—once in a while, it might be lonely at suppertime—but usually I stay so busy and I have friends that are in the same boat, so we'll go out to eat or go to a movie or something."

At the close of our interview, she told me, "My friends laugh at me because they're like, 'You're busier now than when your kids were little!' But I think I just—I find other things to fill my time."

Indeed, while Bethany highlighted her lack of loneliness (except occasionally at suppertime), men more often than women described their feelings using a variant of "lonely." While I did not ask any direct questions about loneliness, over one half of male respondents (51.4%; n=19) but only a little over a tenth of female respondents (11.7%; n=7) used the word "lonely" or "loneliness" to characterize themselves during periods of noncohabitation. For instance, when I asked one male commuter—who, throughout his interview, had spoken very positively about living apart—if there was anything he had not liked about the arrangement, he replied, "Oh, yeah! The travel sucked. Um, y'know, there were times I was very lonely." Similarly, another male interviewee, when asked what he liked least about living apart from his wife, replied, "That's a very good question. Well, I do miss the companionship. I get lonely sometimes. Especially if—in situations when things aren't going well. If I'm ill, or—so, that's—and I'm always traveling." His suggestion that he missed his wife particularly when he was sick aligns with the literature discussed at the beginning of this chapter about women's emotional labor, caring work, and husbands' gains to marriage.

This interviewee's comment also suggests that the physical toll of commuting, discussed in chapter 2, might have a gendered element, if men, more than their wives, were reliant on their partners to perform caring work or to encourage them to seek medical attention. Recall, for instance, the case of Sophie, who suggested that her husband Jay's health might not have deteriorated as much if she had been physically present to tell him, "Hey, you should see a doctor . . . you have to get this checked out." While we should be wary of drawing conclusions based on the small number of individuals who became ill during their commuting periods, it might make sense that husbands would more profoundly experience the health-related impact of living apart, given the literature cited above.

Some of these gender differences are no doubt due to the fact that women in these relationships were more likely than their husbands to live in the family home rather than traveling back and forth to a satellite residence (see appendix A for a description of these arrangements), so they were remaining within preexisting local friendship networks, rather than needing to forge new ones. Further, as discussed, wives were much more likely than husbands to reside with their children, who perhaps in some cases served as a buffer against loneliness. However, even among those who had traveled elsewhere for their jobs, this gender difference remained pronounced; for instance, women commuters more often than men highlighted the importance of the social connections they had made in their new locations. One female respondent, for instance, told me that her new landlady had become a close friend. Another mentioned that she felt "tied to" her house in the place where she worked, adding, "I have a great community of folks. I like my work. I like [this city]."

In a way, this gender difference is not surprising. Previous scholarship has repeatedly pointed out that men's friendship networks, in general, are less salient, intimate, and supportive than women's. (See R. Bell 1981 and Fehr 1996 for extended summaries of this literature.) Researchers have linked these differences to the gender-specific ways in which we are socialized—for instance, the expectation that boys and men should be more emotionally restrained (Bank and Hansford 2000). More specifically, my finding that women commuters, more than men, emphasize their colleagues' social supportiveness, is also in line with prior scholarship. In one 2009 study, for instance, psychologist Rachel Morrison found that women were more likely to emphasize the social and emotional support they gleaned from friendships with colleagues, while men more often discussed how work friends had helped their careers.

The commuter marriage brings these gender differences into sharp focus. Indeed, many female commuters—but few men—emphasized that their social ties become more salient because they were in noncohabiting relationships. As one female respondent succinctly explained, "If anything, my friends became a more important support structure during the time that we were apart."

Lorrie

Lorrie, a professor in her late forties, had been married for nineteen years. Her spouse, who was also a professor, declined to be interviewed for this project. Lorrie told me that she and her husband had lived together for "eight solid years" before getting into a commuting relationship, though their commutes had taken several different shapes over the course of their marriage. At the time I interviewed her, they were living in two different houses located a six-hour drive apart in the same state. According to Lorrie, each spouse thought of their residence as his or her "own." They had a ten-year-old child, who lived with Lorrie.

When I asked whether there was anyone who challenged or judged her living arrangement, Lorrie, like two thirds of respondents (n=64; 66.0%), explained that there were. I then asked if, on the flip side, there was anyone who envied or admired her commuter marriage. To this, Lorrie also replied in the affirmative: "A lot of *women*, I find, get it. And they envy—they get it and it's perfectly clear, the idea of having that kind of space and time to yourself. And the idea of it revitalizing a long-term relationship when you are apart and you get together and you see each other as individuals" (emphasis in original).

Lorrie elaborated on the benefits that time apart could provide. "I think when people are married, they can get into habits and expectations for what the relationship is and what it's going to be," she told me. "I think going to a hotel, to a friend's house, to a family member's house is not something many people are comfortable doing when you're not happy with the behavior of your partner. So when you're trapped in one household, you put up with a lot more crap than you would if you weren't." Lorrie's statement is in line with my finding that cohabitation restricted spouses'—but particularly wives'—"me time," and that living apart disproportionately benefitted women in this way.

Specifically, women commuters more often emphasized the concept of room when discussing what they had gained from living apart. "I love having my own place. I love having space," one woman told me, for instance. Another, similarly, indicated that the greatest benefit of living apart had been "this sense of personal space and time." And when asked what she liked the most about living apart, a different female respondent emphasized, "I have space . . . physical and emotional and private space." While some male commuters made similar comments, these types of responses predominantly came from women.

These responses suggest that there was also a positive dimension to the findings about space and place that I outlined in chapter 2. As discussed, spouses could feel disconnected in these relationships, and communication technologies—while useful—were not enough to completely bridge that separation. However, the ability to disconnect could also be a benefit of this lifestyle.

"You Are So Lucky": Gender and Envy

Female respondents were more likely than male respondents to agree that others might admire or envy their relationships. Among the ninety re-spondents who answered the question "Were there any people who en-vied you or admired your living situation?" 70.9 percent (n=39) of female commuters responded in the affirmative, compared to only 34.2 percent (n=12) of men.[2] Moreover, many female commuters, like Lorrie above, emphasized that it was women who admired or envied their lifestyle. As the three responses below—and the many others like them from female commuters—illuminate, respondents made this connection even though they were not specifically asked about gender differences in others' reac-tions to their relationships. The bolded emphases are mine:

> *Were there any people who envied you or admired your living situation?*
> I think I actually have a lot of **women friends** that are incredibly envious. And for whatever reason feel that they've got partners or husbands who would not be supportive of that kind of a situation. I think that **women** often yearn for *their* [emphasis in original] space and for privacy some-times. And in many ways, my taking the job in [this city] has afforded us each a space that maybe we wouldn't have had if I had found work in the area [where my husband lives]. And so I think that there [are]—**women, more than men**, from my impression and perception—who tend to be a little envious and who tend to admire, as well.
> Yes! Most every **mother** of teenagers that I know envies me. Seriously. I mean, maybe they're just being glib. But I've gotten so many comments like, 'Oh my God, you're living the mid-life crisis dream. What I would give to have my own place in [the city]!'
> Oh, yeah. All of my friends—I was the last of my friends, my high school [and] college friends, to make a commitment to somebody. And the ones who've been together for twenty-five or thirty years will say, 'Oh my God, I would love my own apartment. You are so lucky.' Whether they have kids that are driving them crazy or a husband who is driving them crazy. But all—**especially my women friends**, *all* of them [emphasis in

original] who have been married more than twenty years will say to me, 'You're so lucky having your own apartment. I wish I did.'

Again, I did not initially ask interviewees about which gender of person was more likely to envy their relationships, which makes the specific emphasis on women's envy particularly compelling. By discussing the envy their lifestyle incurred, particularly in female acquaintances, commuter spouses brought into sharp focus the loss of "me time" experienced disproportionately by cohabitating wives more generally.

Indeed, when I asked follow-up questions of these respondents, they were reflective about gender and marriage, in ways that directly connected with the "leisure gap" literature. For example, Myra—a respondent in her mid-forties who worked in an administrative position at a college—had been married for twenty years and noncohabitating for only a few months when I interviewed her. She told me that when she had initially thought about living apart from her husband, she had assumed she would feel guilty, though her female friends indicated that she might enjoy it: "You [think you] should feel guilty or you should feel that it's a situation of lack somehow. So I think I was just processing all that. I didn't go right to that place that [my female friends] went. But after they said that, I definitely considered it. I thought, 'Yeah, maybe I will enjoy it.' And now I just told you I am definitely enjoying it for sure. I've claimed it. Those nights are great. [*laughs*]"

Toward the end of our interview, Myra, like many of my interviewees, asked if I could share some of the ongoing findings from my study with her. We chatted about how other commuters, too, had told me that females expressed an envy of these arrangements. She indicated that this did not surprise her:

And what does that say? Culturally, we sort of know what it says with the exception of a few real Mr. Moms and really unusually supportive partners, it's the equivalent of what people say about Black History Month or something. When you have an appointed, sort of special time out, what that tells you is that the norm is—it's not included there. So that's what 'girls' night out' is. It's like this common thing. And I've noticed in our neighborhood that it's a very suburban thing that I have noticed over the years means working moms—or even stay-at-home moms—who don't think that they can regularly just do things that they want to do. They formalize this thing called 'girls' night out,' where you get one night and you get to go do something. [*laughs*]

To be clear, it was not only women who engaged in this discourse about envy, but it was disproportionately women. Furthermore, while two male respondents specifically indicated that their male friends were jealous of their arrangements, other male respondents also talked about how women envied their commuter lifestyles. For instance, when I asked Ethan if he felt others challenged or judged his relationship, he replied, "People who are closest to us get it. People, depending on their profession, get it. You know, academics like you get it. That's academia, you know? And people who are accountants don't get it. People who work for the government don't get it. Most *women* I know are totally envious of what I describe" (emphasis in original).

In sum, these narratives about living apart as a kind of respite were gendered in ways that tie into previous literature both about men and women in long-distance relationships and about gender and the benefits of marriage more generally. In the previous chapter, I discussed how some women commuters described their arrangements as a kind of "hall pass" from the demands of domestic femininity. But these relationships also represented a "hall pass" from constant companionship, and this had its positive dimensions. As one female respondent explained, "There was definitely a sense of freedom" in living apart. "And there's a certain bit of refreshment to that."

Caveats and Limitations

After I shared an early draft of this chapter with a male colleague, he suggested that male respondents might be reticent to talk to me, a female researcher, about how much they enjoyed being away from their wives, while women respondents might be more upfront. While it is possible that my gender did come into play in the way he was suggesting, I remain confident in this chapter's findings for several reasons. First, as discussed further in appendix A, I used techniques to encourage truthful responses.

Additionally, the men in my sample were seemingly quite forthcoming with me about other intimate details of their relationships—for instance, arguments with their wives and their sex lives, the latter of which I did not even ask about directly. One male commuter told me that he used to go on drinking binges during the period he lived apart from his wife, and that she still does not know about that. My findings were also internally consistent. For instance, while women respondents discussed the importance of their social ties, men more often talked about being lonely. Finally, not only do these findings make sense in the context of the literature on male and female benefits to marriage, but, as discussed, they are also consistent with prior scholarship on commuter spouses and other long-distance relationships.

Another potential limitation of these findings is that, in looking at broader gendered trends, I flatten some of the heterogeneity in responses. For instance, some women (seven, in fact) discussed their loneliness when their husbands were away, and a few men told me that they enjoyed the break from their wives. Asked what he liked best about his commuting arrangement, for instance, one male respondent replied, "I don't feel as hemmed in—and maybe that's not the right word, maybe that's not the kindest way to characterize other people's choices but I feel I have a sort of extra measure of freedom that I secretly think some of my peers sort of envy." His description of feeling "hemmed in" by cohabitation is squarely in line with the narrative about space that was characteristic of female respondents. While such responses were the exceptions, not the rule, it is important to acknowledge these outliers in order to get a full picture of the lived experiences of commuters.

Another caveat: in this chapter, I have traced some potential benefits of this lifestyle that seem to disproportionately impact wives—and drawbacks that seem to disproportionately impact husbands. However, this does not mean that commuting was the ideal or preferred lifestyle, for either husbands or wives. As I emphasize throughout this book, my interviewees lived apart from their spouses because of the conflicting demands of their jobs—not because they felt this arrangement suited them better. Lydia, for instance, who was quoted above saying that living apart lets you do "the selfish things" that you do not get to do in the presence of your spouse, qualified her statement later in the interview: "Now, that said, if we had the opportunity to live together 100 percent of the time with no inconvenience to our jobs, we'd certainly take that over the current arrangement." Indeed, when asked if they planned to resume cohabitation with their spouses in the future, if they had not already done so, all but one respondent indicated that they did.

At the same time, the people I interviewed were quite forthcoming about the benefits they did reap from their arrangements, even as they saw these arrangements as nonideal. As Brianna, a medical fellow in her mid-thirties who had resumed cohabitation, explained about living apart, "I would have more independence and, you know, I would be able to decide what I was doing on weekends on the few weekends I was there and he wasn't, and I wasn't on-call, but it still would've been better to have him there."

Conclusions

Historically, one of the advantages of heterosexual marriage for men has been their access to expressive emotive support—and, indeed, research still suggests that this is more important for husbands than wives. At the same time, scholars have highlighted a recently emerged deficit in both duration and quality of leisure time among wives and mothers. Based on both literatures, it makes sense that—at least in some ways—women would have an edge and men would be at a disadvantage in relationships where the couple does not always live together. My female interviewees had access to some of the benefits of heterosexual marriage (such as financial pooling) while also having access to additional free time and personal space. My male respondents may have been more likely to feel lonely not only because they lost immediate access to women's emotion-work but also because they generally did not have the same types of social support structures as their wives.

Of course, men also provide emotional support, women also get lonely, and some men have strong friendship networks while some women do not. But, overall, the way that male and female commuters across my sample talked about living apart was markedly different, and these differences shed light on what heterosexual relationships—and, particularly, cohabitation—have to offer men and women more generally. As Gerstel and Gross summarized in their 1984 study of commuter spouses, "These commuters, married yet single for much of the time, are in a position to tell us what marriage—with its members' daily proximity—both provides and denies" (52).

Interestingly, while much has changed since 1984 when it comes to the gendered dimensions of American marriage, and marriage may not benefit men in the same ways as it once did, my findings regarding the particular advantages of commuting for women were strikingly similar to Gerstel and Gross's. Despite broader shifts in gender roles, women's increased presence in the workforce, and the ability to connect instantly (barring technological snafus) through FaceTime, email, texting, and Skype, some of the ways in which people experience gender in these relationships have remained quite static over time. In aligning with decades-old work on commuter spouses, the findings in this chapter shed light on the durability of gendered meanings and roles more broadly—for instance, the enduring stereotype of the wife as the emotional laborer and the differences in men's and women's friendship structures. These findings also align with more recent work on the leisure gap by suggesting that women more profoundly experience noncohabitation as a boon to their "me time."

At first glance, these leisure differences may seem trivial. Of what social consequence is it that a man may have access to more "me time" while a woman may need to go out of her way to plan a "girls' night out"? Yet these disparities have broader social meaning and importance. Indeed, sociologist Susan Shaw (2001), who has argued that "leisure practices are linked to power and power relations in society," directly positions the concept of a mother taking leisure time as an act of resistance (186). For Shaw, ideologies that support the gender-power hierarchy underlie asymmetrical leisure practices. In forging these particular arrangements, commuter spouses—whether intentionally or not—disrupt that hierarchy.

It is also particularly noteworthy that commuter spouses, as a group, reflect these gendered trends. We might expect to find a high degree of individualism and gender equality in these marriages—points I have both supported and problematized in previous chapters. Indeed, as discussed, commuter spouses themselves often speak about being quite independent. So the fact that even these already individualistic, egalitarian people experience their separation as a boon to their personal freedom is quite telling. Recall the words of Bethany, quoted at the beginning of this chapter: "What do I like the most? Well I can pretty much do whatever I want. . . .

And I do anyway, when he's here or not here it doesn't really matter." Despite the fact that she can do "whatever" she wants when her husband is in the house, she still highlights the fact that noncohabitation impacts her autonomy. In short, my findings in this chapter suggest that when it comes to "me time," cohabitation matters in a way that is gendered.

Finally, in this chapter I have looked at how wives and husbands may experience commuter marriages differently, and how that relates to the benefits and drawbacks of marriage and cohabitation for women and men more broadly. But there are other potential stakeholders in commuter marriage beyond the spouses. For instance, as discussed in chapter 2, some commuters suggested that their children benefited from these arrangements in some ways—in terms of increased independence, for instance—although many parents also worried about the negative impact of these relationships on their children.

Additionally, one might argue that employers benefit from commuter marriage, as it provides them with access to Acker's (1990) "disembodied" employees, who are detached from their families and focused on their careers. Indeed, as discussed in the last chapter, when I asked respondents if there was anything they liked about their commuting arrangements, the most common answer was that they were able to be more productive at work. At the same time, it is unclear whether these arrangements are ideal for employers in the long term, compared to the alternatives. For instance, commuter spouses may have lower workplace affinity than other workers. Indeed, many of the people I interviewed were in fixed-term positions or indicated that they actively looked for positions closer to their spouses. Some commuters mentioned that they were deliberately vague to their employers about their family arrangements in order to avoid being branded as uncommitted.

For the commuters themselves, however, clearly there were some advantages to these relationships, even if living apart was not their preferred arrangement. In the next chapter, I delve more explicitly into their feelings about the positive and negative aspects of these relationships, focusing on the question I most often get asked about commuter spouses: "Are they happy?"

6

"But Are They Happy?"

*I was having dinner with a scholar who was visiting my university to give
a talk. As I buttered my roll, I told her I was working on a book about
spouses who lived apart for their jobs. "So what's going on with them?"
she asked. "Are they happy doing that?"*

This is the question I get asked most often about commuter spouses—by
colleagues, family members, friends, neighbors, and, once, a stranger in
the post office line: "Are they happy?" (Variations have included "Is it
difficult?," "Do they like it?," and "Do they love it or hate it?").[1] For the
most part, people seem to be interested in these couples whose lives are
dissimilar to their own—and, specifically, in the viability of these alternative arrangements. Interestingly, many commuter spouses themselves ask
me the same question. They often express a desire to gauge how typical
(or "normal") their own experiences have been.

To be clear, while I did ask commuters what they enjoyed or did not
enjoy about these relationships, their satisfaction with living apart was not
the primary focus of this project. When I began this study, I was primarily

interested in commuter spouses not because of how they negotiated the dynamics of these unusual relationships (although that was interesting, too), but because of how their particular arrangements might shed light on broader social patterns and changes in cultural norms. There has already been significant scholarship on the benefits and pitfalls of long-distance relationships more generally. For example, research in counseling psychology has indicated that these relationships are characterized by stress (Groves and Horm-Wingerd 1991; Rhodes 2002). Additional research has linked noncohabitation to a diminution in emotional support, decreased physical intimacy, and the decreased ability of individuals to "make sense" of their relationships (Gerstel and Gross 1984, 47); to dissatisfaction with family life, with one's relationship, and with life as a whole (Bunker et al. 1992); to dissatisfaction both with time spent together and with affectional communication (Govaerts and Dixon 1988); to loneliness, increased financial costs, and adverse reactions from others (Magnuson and Norem 1999); and even to "low-grade mental illness" (Bennett 2007). Previous research has also pointed to the advantages associated with noncohabitation. For example, couples living apart are more satisfied with their work lives and the time they have for themselves (Bunker et al. 1992).

Despite the fact that measuring commuters' contentment was not the primary objective of this project, my interviews aligned with this prior work in that they revealed noncohabitation to be a double-edged sword. Were the commuters I interviewed "happy" in these relationships? Yes . . . and no. Clearly, though commuter spouses perceived some benefits to these relationships, they experienced real challenges as a result of their noncohabitation. I have detailed both of these aspects of commuter marriages in this book. For instance, while some spouses felt that being physically apart had improved the quality of their communication (chapter 1), many indicated that noncohabitation presented new challenges for communicating, and that new technologies such as texting and Skype were not a substitute for physical copresence (chapter 2). In some ways these arrangements were egalitarian, though other ways they exacerbated inequalities, such as gender differences in time spent on childcare (chapter 4). Many commuters, particularly women, found that these lifestyles enabled them to be more productive at work (chapter 4) and gave them more freedom (chapter 5). Still, while living apart gave spouses additional "me time," alleviating some of the mundanity and tension associated with coresidence, it could also produce loneliness (chapter 5). Many commuters encountered judgment from friends and family for their lifestyles (chapter 3). There were potentially some negative health implications of these relationships as well (chapter 2). In all, while elements of these relationships could be rewarding, for the most part commuters did not perceive their arrangements as optimal. Indeed, many did not interpret commuter marriage as something that they had willingly chosen, instead focusing on the external constraints that had made living apart a "necessity" (chapter 3).

Reunited and It Feels So . . . Good?

Those spouses who had already resumed cohabitation were particularly reflective about the relative advantages and disadvantages of living apart. While they generally said that their preference was to live together, some also discussed the challenges that arose when they resumed cohabitation.

This finding aligns with research on other types of geographically separate couples, which has also discussed the potential friction created by reunification. As Dinah Hannaford (2017) puts it, in her work on transnational Senegalese spouses in financial remittance relationships, "For couples that have spent a large part of their married life living separately, reuniting can represent a new form of 'everyday ruptures' (Coe 2011) caused by migration rather than a resolution of rupture" (109). Research on postdeployment reunification has found that military spouses face some similar challenges. "Although homecoming should be a joyous time for military couples," one study observes, "the reentry of a service member into the family can be more challenging than deployment itself" (Knobloch and Theiss 2012, 423). Though commuter spouses do not have to deal with the added challenges that can come along with reunification after a military deployment (for instance, how to reintegrate the soldier into civilian life), like post-deployment military couples, reuniting commuters must cede some of the autonomy associated with living apart. According to my respondents, one of the difficulties arose in navigating space, particularly when the couple now shared a residence that one spouse had previously occupied alone. As one former commuter told me, "We actually got into it when we started living together because I didn't feel like it was at all my house when I moved in." This aligns with literature suggesting that military spouses may experience "heightened conflict" when they again share a home (Knobloch and Theiss 2012, 432; see also Theiss and Knobloch 2014).

In another quite interesting case, a commuter couple had lived apart, reunited, gotten divorced, and were now remarried to each other only to be living apart again. Though they said they did not necessarily enjoy living apart, they had also seen the pitfalls of reunification up close. As the wife in this couple explained:

> One thing we have discovered—when we moved back in . . . together—we didn't have a problem living apart, I mean we missed each other and all, but when we moved back in together, that was when we really struggled. We actually separated and were divorced for six months and then remarried on what would have been our tenth anniversary. And one of the things we realized then was that, we felt like we reached this point where all we were ever doing was compromising on everything and neither of us really getting what we wanted. So one of the things we've always done since then is, everywhere we live, we each have our own office. We each have one space that we can keep as messy as we want, we can decorate however we want. It's kind of like the room of one's own. And then the rest of the house is negotiated, and you don't leave your mess there. . . . And that's worked really well. My 'second husband' is *great*. [*laughs*] [emphasis in original]
> *If you don't mind telling me, what are some of the things you struggled with when you moved back together?*
> I think it was that living apart, we had really kind of gone into our own routines and how we really wanted things to be, and when we moved back in together we were compromising again and feeling a little more frustrated with the compromises . . .

I asked if she could give me an example of something on which she felt they were both compromising. She responded: "Yeah, so for example, you're gonna buy a couch. And, you know, I like the black couch. He likes the white couch. So we compromise and get the grey couch. So neither one of us were getting exactly what we wanted, and we realized that at certain points—well, it's the kind of thing where I don't care enough about the color of the couch to fight to the death on it. It isn't worth having a fight about. But we've kind of both learned more that—to kind of go, okay, these are the things that I just want to be the one to have the control of this decision. For this time. Unless the other one really hates it." Relearning how to negotiate these kinds of compromises in a shared space was one of the major challenges for the reunited commuters in my sample.

Further, even some respondents who had not resumed cohabitation said that they anticipated challenges when that day came. "Well, as both of us being essentially geo-bachelors, we run our own schedules and do whatever we want. Once we're actually living together it'll be a little bit harder," one male respondent told me, adding, "You're used to doing things your own way, and then suddenly you're not." Some respondents took these concerns relatively seriously. One woman, for instance, explained that she was "nervous" about their relationship dynamics upon reunification, adding in a worried voice, "I'm just not sure if it's going to work out." Others were a bit lighthearted about such potential issues. A female respondent, for instance, laughingly told me that the couple's retirement years "might be harder than we think!" She said that she and her husband might need to "have rules about how long the TV can be on for, and who has the kitchen during certain parts of the day and how loud the radio can be," though she quickly added, "Generally these things, we joke about them but they don't create any big problems when we're together. So I don't anticipate any problems when we retire."

These potential challenges of reunification provide evidence that living apart can reduce or eliminate some everyday tensions—for instance, related to housework (who does the laundry?), leisure time (who gets the remote?), and sex (how often?)—that might otherwise exist in a cohabitating relationship. "I think the aftermath has been interesting," explained one respondent, who had since resumed cohabitation with her husband. "One of the positives about being apart is that a lot of the basis for daily conflict is removed."[2] Still, it bears repeating that *all* respondents, except for one, were either living with their spouses again or indicated that they anticipated eventually living together. Though there were some elements of living apart that provided pleasure, few respondents were happier in these arrangements. As Al succinctly put it, "[Commuting has] been fine, it's worked out, but I'm kind of looking forward to when it's over."

"Are They Happy?": Variation among Commuters

While in this book I have primarily emphasized overarching patterns in how my respondents discussed their experiences of living apart, in each chapter I have also highlighted outliers and variation among commuters. There was heterogeneity in how my respondents discussed their happiness with these arrangements as well. A few said that they were on the brink of divorce, and at least three respondents cried on the phone with me. At the other end of the spectrum, some enthusiastically told me that perhaps all married couples should give noncohabitation a try. It also became clear that how commuters felt about these relationships varied based on elements such as their job types, the structures of their commutes, the presence or absence of children, and their places in the life course.

First, respondents with different types of jobs had different things to say about their satisfaction with these relationships. Those who worked in academia, for instance, seemed to have some structural advantages. In particular, professors emphasized that the relative flexibility of their work schedules and the long winter and summer breaks, during which they could work remotely, made these relationships more tenable.

Commuters also discussed how the circumstances of their specific relationships—for instance, how far apart they lived, how often they were able to see each other, and how often they talked to their spouses—played a role in their contentment (or lack thereof) with these arrangements. Those who lived relatively far apart and who were able to see each other less frequently often discussed these circumstances as sources of frustration. Moreover, as I have discussed, although most people I interviewed were white collar workers who had communication technologies readily available (as compared to other types of long-distance spouses, such as oil rig workers), those who lived in different time zones from their spouses reported that as a barrier to communication and to their overall satisfaction with their arrangements. Recall, for instance, Wade, profiled in chapter 2, who had difficulty coordinating communication with his wife because of their fifteen-hour time difference.

Finally, perhaps the most important element that seemed to impact how commuters felt about their relationships was parenthood. I have discussed how having young children can exacerbate the strains of separation and introduce additional complications into these relationships.[3] For instance, couples with minor children experienced conflict over gender roles related to caretaking, and they often had the added worry about the impact of their separation upon their children. Perhaps unsurprisingly, those commuters most content with their relationships seemed to be couples without children, or those with grown children who had already left the nest.

Some of the relatively young couples in my sample said that living apart was something that they were able to do because of their stage in life, as they planned to resume cohabitation before having children. One respondent, for example, was pregnant at the time of our interview. The baby was due after the completion of her fixed-term position, at which point she would have already returned to the house she shared with her husband. This timeline, she told me, was "very by design." As I discussed in chapter 2, some interviewees without children spontaneously mentioned that they would not have undertaken this lifestyle if they'd been parents. And recall Bethany, from the previous chapter, who indicated that she thought others envied the commuting lifestyle—with the caveat "unless you have little kids."

Advice for Potential Commuters

My interviewees also highlighted the importance of parental status and stage in life when they discussed what words of wisdom they might offer to potential commuters. At the end of each interview, I asked, "Do you have any advice for other couples who are thinking about living apart?" One of the salient themes that arose in response to this question was the importance of being in the right phase of a relationship. Again, many respondents cautioned that having children made this lifestyle trickier than it might otherwise be. "Don't do it if you have kids!" one respondent advised, for instance (he had kids).

Others emphasized factors that were not necessarily specific to life course but related to the overall quality of the relationship. Some commuters indicated that there was a "type" of person or relationship that was particularly suited to this lifestyle. Dovetailing with my argument in chapter 1, some suggested that people who were individualistic and "not too dependent" (as one respondent put it) on their partners would fare better in these relationships. Moreover, some indicated that potential commuters should make sure the marriage was on a firm footing—that they should "get the relationship in order" and "not have major problems"—before attempting something like this. Indeed, prior literature and my findings seem to suggest that this final piece of advice has merit. As discussed in chapter 2, when a relationship is going well, it can be more easily maintained through "sunny day" (Wilding 2006, 134) technologies such as email, text messages, phone calls, and video chat. However, when major issues arise, communication technologies are not a substitute for proximity, and living apart can complicate those issues.

There were several other common themes in response to the request for advice as well. About one in ten respondents (n=10) used the word "flexible" or "flexibility" in response to this question, suggesting that potential commuters should not have rigid expectations about how these arrangements would operate. "As long as you're flexible in your expectations and your relationship is strong, you are not going to have a problem," one interviewee explained, for example. Other responses were varied, with some commuters doling out logistical advice related to communication or traveling ("Make sure you get your miles on Amtrak so you can go to the club. And make sure you're nice to the person at the desk"). Others were more cynical. "Oh boy," one male respondent replied to this question, "good luck. [*laughs*] You know. I would sort of say, 'Get ready to be lonely. Get ready to feel lonely.'" Later in the interview, when discussing some of the perks of the new locations where he had lived for his jobs, this respondent added, "[But] I've never gotten a position and, before going, thought how wonderful it was going to be. It's always hard. It's never easy. It's never fun. It's never, 'I can't wait to get out of here and get to there.' It's always, 'Well, I have to endure this and we will get through it the best we can.'" Along these lines, another common response to the request for advice was, "Don't do it."

Still, when giving advice, commuters for the most part were hopeful, not only about what was in store for their own relationships but about how their experiences might help others. "I wish someone had given *me* advice!" one respondent told me. Another commuter explained, "I think one of the hardest things about being apart—not for our actual marriage, but for me as an individual—is that so few other people understand it. There's not a lot of shared experience. And like I said, I think that's why when I saw you were doing research, I was like, 'Oh! Someone actually cares!'" Many of my respondents expressed a desire to see the results of this study, to learn about others' experiences, and potentially to help others by sharing their own stories. I periodically send them updates on my research via email, and some still correspond with me regularly, letting me know what is happening in their lives. Though it was not the primary intent of this project, it is my hope that commuter spouses find the stories and discussions in this book to be illuminating, and that potential commuters might use them to become better informed about the nuances of this lifestyle.

The main emphasis of this study has not been what commuter spouses themselves gain or lose from these arrangements—rather, how their lifestyles might shed light on broader social forces and historical trends. Yet the way that commuter spouses talk about their level of contentment with these relationships itself illuminates some of these overarching trends. The different experiences of women and men when it comes to satisfaction in these relationships, for instance, shed light on the persistence of gendered expectations and roles more generally. Commuters' communication-related frustrations problematize the notion of "the death of distance" (Cairncross 1997, 5), suggesting that, while new technologies have fundamentally changed our experiences with non-face-to-face communication, they are still not substitutes for physical proximity. The finding that commuters seem to be more satisfied with the amount of work they produce when living apart is illustrative of a broader mismatch between family roles and occupational expectations, particularly for women.

This book has been about dual-earning professionals who live apart from their spouses due to their jobs. Throughout these pages, I have outlined these commuters' experiences of living apart—how they feel about their marriages, how they remain in touch, and how they think it impacts their children and their working lives. However, this book has not only been about dual-earning professionals who live apart from their spouses due to their jobs. I have also emphasized that these relatively privileged, married couples are a strategic population poised to shed light on broader social dynamics. These dynamics include cultural shifts in the meaning of marriage and the family (chapter 1), the implications of technology use on intimate relationships (chapter 2), the changing structure and meaning of professional work (chapter 3), and the changing—though, in many ways static—gender norms and roles related to work, marriage, and the family (chapters 4 and 5). I have argued that these couples are in a unique position to understand and articulate the often-conflicting relationship between family and work, as they go through periods of apartness and togetherness. Next, in the conclusion, I further trace and extend these arguments.

Conclusion

I'm finishing this book on the floor of a vacant house while waiting for a contractor to arrive. After completing my fellowship at Vanderbilt, I took a short-term job at another institution and finally, two years ago, accepted a tenure-track job as a professor at my current university. I live with my husband and daughter but I commute an hour and a half each way to campus—the kind of drive that means you end up knowing, and maybe even starting to love, the lyrics to awful Nickelback songs from the early 2000s. I sing along loudly, licking my fingers—fast-food ketchup carnage on the steering wheel. Relatives cluck at me sympathetically about the commute now, just as they did when my husband and I lived apart, but I tell them I enjoy my alone time, and I mean it. It's the one time of day when no one asks anything from me, except the robotic voice on Waze, and I recognize that in the current academic job market I am fortunate to have this arrangement.

Our family rented an apartment for a few years, unsure of what the future would hold, as I slowly grew roots in my new position and my husband took a job as an attorney in New Jersey. We began to sway, more and more comfortably, to the rhythm of our new roles as workers and parents. Now we've bought a home and will move around the time the final edits of this book are due. If you open the book, newly bought, it's probably crisp and pristine in ivory and black with perhaps the faint odor of fresh printing. What you don't see are the bumps and creases representing the stops and starts that I took as I tackled other projects and made my own life transitions. There is no trace of the fact that I began the background research for chapter 1 in a tiny Nashville apartment or that part of chapter 3 was written in a NICU while waiting for my underweight preemie to be released from the hospital. Those invisible markings are a roadmap to the sinewy curves of my life as I've attempted to reconcile work, family, and geography.

This is not a Disney ending for us—a narrative cradled in a beautiful bow. There are still many "what ifs" looming on the horizon. What if something happens to my husband's company? What if I don't get tenure? What if the public schools here are not a good fit for our child? What if? These are the hypotheticals of privileged people, to be sure, but they are nonetheless revealing. We are "settled" with an asterisk. We will sink back into our couches (once we get couches) still feeling the uneasiness now attached to professional work in the contingent, postindustrial economy. For the time being, though, I stare out at the blank room ahead of me and just look forward to being able to put pictures on my walls.

Every commuter I interviewed for this book has a story that, like mine, is unique and nuanced. As a sociologist, it is often difficult to capture overarching patterns in human behavior while also attending to the rich variation in the lived experiences of individuals. Throughout this book, I have attempted to bring out some of those personal details, to the extent that it is possible while maintaining my participants' anonymity. At the same time, while this book is a collection of individual stories, it is also about how those stories are shaped by and illuminate broader social forces. In the introduction, I indicated that the material in this book intersects with and extends broader sociological scholarship in three central areas: the shift toward individualization in marriage, changing gender dynamics at home and at work (and at the intersection of the two), and the changing structure and meaning of professional work. Below, I trace how my findings have contributed to sociological theory and to empirical research in these areas, as well as how these findings might inform future research, institutional policies, and practice.

Contributions to Theory

Over the course of the book, I have contextualized commuter marriages within several different theoretical literatures; commuter spouses, in turn, complicate and extend these existing theories. In chapter 1, for instance, I explore how commuter couples are relevant to Giddens's (1992) notion of the "pure relationship," in which "a social relation is entered into for its own sake, for what can be derived by each person from a sustained association with another; and which is continued only in so far as it is thought by both parties to deliver enough satisfactions for each individual to stay within it" (58). While I qualify that Giddens did not view the "pure relationship" as being attached to marriage or any other social institution, I demonstrate that commuter marriages are very close to "pure" in some ways. At the same time, I illustrate how, even in these highly individualized relationships, commitment to the dyad remains strong. Indeed, I suggest that, in part, this collectivist ideology may arise precisely because these relationships are individualized in a nonnormative way. While the "pure relationship" is a relevant theoretical frame for considering contemporary Western relationships, commuter spouses illuminate some stumbling blocks to the realization of this vision.

I have also argued that commuter spouses are a useful empirical context for analyzing theories of space and distance. In chapter 2, I demonstrate how my respondents embody Lefebvre's ([1991] 2014) notion that social and mental space are entities distinct from physical space. At the same time, these couples' descriptions of their relationships also align with prior literature about the "death of distance"—specifically, the notion that advancement in communication technology "loosens" but does not eliminate "the grip of geography" (Cairncross 1997, 5). My respondents are particularly poised to illustrate the "death of distance" because they are, for the most part, white-collar workers with ready access to the latest gadgets. Yet even for these relatively privileged individuals, distance has not relaxed its grip. Physical space still matters and cannot be fully bridged, even through "constant" contact across a range of devices.

This analysis of commuter marriage has contributed to theoretical scholarship on deviance as well. In particular, as I argue in chapter 3, commuter spouses help us to more broadly conceptualize the notion of "strain" (Merton 1938; 1968). My respondents' narratives about their lack of choice demonstrate how even relatively privileged individuals can feel squeezed into nonnormative arrangements by structural constraints and cultural demands—in this case, by the mismatch between the structures of professional work and family, combined with late-capitalist notions of economic necessity and extreme "devotion" (Blair-Loy 2009) to their careers.

Finally, my findings here enhance gender theory. For instance, prior literature has explored how gender is constructed and reconstructed through daily, routinized social interactions (Berk 1985; West and Zimmerman 1987) as well as how everyday microlevel interactions might undermine the gender-power structure (Butler 2004; Deutsch 2007; Risman 2009). This theoretical scholarship on "doing" and "undoing" gender informs my analysis in chapter 4. Yet my analysis informs and extends that theory as well. As Risman (2009) has suggested, "Doing gender research would be improved by more attention to undoing gender" (81). I attend to that here. By focusing on a nontraditional and potentially egalitarian relationship form, this book has unveiled one empirical context where spouses in heterosexual marriages engage in potentially subversive gendered performances. For instance, the commuting arrangement facilitates role-segmentation for some women, enabling them to detach home and work and become hyperproductive, stereotypically "male" (Acker 1990) workers. However, my analysis has also highlighted "the doing"—the persistence of normative gendered performances—as I discuss further below.

In addition to engaging with theoretical scholarship, my findings have provided contributions to existing empirical literatures, particularly in the thematic areas I discuss in the next three sections.

The Cultural Shift toward (Marital) Individualization

The disjuncture between the individual and the collective, particularly within the institution of marriage, is one thread I have woven throughout the book. In chapter 1, I summarized how the shift toward individualization exists in tension with traditional notions about marriage. I explained how commuter marriages are a particularly interesting site at which to analyze that tension, since the partners live in separate residences but remain married. In many ways, commuter spouses are the poster children for individualized marriage, as they live apart in service to their personal career aspirations. Indeed, my respondents did emphasize their autonomy. As discussed in chapter 2, some even said they hoped that this arrangement would make their offspring more self-sufficient as well. Clearly, they prized independence as a positive quality.

However, as explored throughout the book, commuter spouses also described themselves as quite enmeshed with their partners. As I discussed in chapter 1, they emphasized how often they relied on each other both for emotional support and for practical purposes, particularly for childcare—and, as I discuss further in chapter 5, for financial support. Whether or not these couples really did rely on each other in practice, these narratives about interreliance suggest the salience of collectivist paradigms, even for these seemingly highly autonomous spouses. In these marriages, the two partners continued to think of themselves as a unit despite living separately.

This collectivist orientation also came out in the way they discussed their residences. As explored in chapter 2, commuters in "satellite" relationships often thought of the residence they shared with their partners as home, regardless of how much time they personally spent living there. Further, as discussed in chapter 3, some of them indicated that living apart was a move to strengthen their families in the long run.

Finally, communication technologies facilitated these spouses' sense of continual enmeshment. As discussed throughout the book and again above, contrary to commuter spouses in earlier studies and to some other types of long-distance couples, my respondents had the ability to feel constantly in contact through mechanisms such as texting, email, and Skype. As I explore in chapter 2, they designated different modes of communication as buckets for different types of information in their lives—for instance, the phone for emotional conversations and emails for more bureaucratic tasks—and to sustain their feelings of interdependence. Some spouses even declared that they communicated more extensively when they were apart than together. These findings not only contribute to the marital individualization literature, demonstrating how new modes of communication can help facilitate emotional and task-based interdependence, even for highly independent partners. They also contribute to prior literature in the communications field. For instance, they reflect the contention that such technologies can facilitate "hyperpersonal" interaction (Walther 1996, 5), and they illuminate the potentials and pitfalls of technology for sustaining intimate relationships more broadly.

In sum, commuter spouses represent both the push of individualization and the pull of collectivist ideals. By embodying both the current propelling us forward and the ties that lash us to the past, these couples inform our understanding of changing cultural meanings surrounding marriage in the United States and elsewhere.

Changing Gender Dynamics at Home and Work

One major component of the literature on individualization is the notion that this historical trend dovetails with increasingly egalitarian gender roles within heterosexual marriage. Further, extensive research on the sociology of gender has focused on women's changing roles in the workforce and the domestic sphere, and the intersection between the two. I began the book suggesting that these couples might be instructive as extreme examples of women's increased presence in the labor force and the democratization of gender roles at home.

Indeed, I found support for this idea. In chapter 4, for instance, I described how commuter spouses are able to subvert gender expectations in some ways. The most obvious way is by assigning importance to the woman's career, to the extent that it disrupts the normative structure of family life. Further, as indicated above, in some cases the wives in these relationships are able to work in a "male" way (Acker 1990), disentangling domestic and professional obligations. As I demonstrated in chapter 5, women commuters also seem to more profoundly experience the freedoms of living apart. They appear to be more apt to make and rely upon social connections beyond their spouses, while men more often report feeling lonely in these marriages. That is, women appear to gain from the individualized features of these marriages in some gender-specific ways—

ways that have been true since researchers began studying this topic in the 1980s and that persist today. In some ways, commuter marriages are indeed illuminating contexts where gender can work differently.

However, as discussed in chapter 4, gender in these relationships is a stuck zipper; it is not fully undone. Normative gender roles play out in these marriages just as they do in cohabitating relationships, with perhaps the most extreme example being the division of childcare. As I have explored in chapter 3, the stigmatization of this lifestyle also appears to be gendered, in ways that play into traditional conceptions about men, women, family roles, and work. Unlike some other types of long-distance relationships, commuter marriage challenges normative conceptions of what it means to be a "good wife" and, in some cases, a "good mother," but commuters encounter the gendered backlash that comes along with that. In line with prior research (e.g., Bergen 2010a, 2010b; M. Holmes 2004b), I found that women commuters more often than men said that they encountered social disapproval of their lifestyle. In sum, by exploring these couples' dynamics, I have contributed to existing literature on gender in two key ways: both by illuminating a subversive context and by illustrating the entrenchment of these gendered dynamics even in this nonnormative case.

The Changing Structure and Meaning of Professional Work

Why do commuter spouses live apart? Exploring this question throughout the book, I have suggested that the answer is both structural and cultural. The way that contemporary professional work is organized—and, particularly, the broader shift toward the contingent economy—clearly plays a large role in these relationships. In chapter 3, I have demonstrated how prior research on the sociology of deviance has highlighted the structural constraints that squeeze individuals into nonnormative arrangements. My respondents, though ostensibly privileged in many ways, also felt that squeeze. As discussed in chapter 6, these couples did not opt into commuting as a lifestyle preference. Most of their rationales for living apart seemed to hang someplace in the balance between choice and compulsion. Some were content in the arrangements, some were miserable, and many more existed someplace in between, but the vast majority (all except one) stated that reunification was their end goal.

At the same time, these commuters' entrenched occupational role-identities also helped to drive their nonnormative arrangements. Of course, workers of all types may experience difficulty reconciling work and family demands, and all have their agency constrained by structural forces in some way or another. Yet my findings specifically illuminate the concept of "professional necessity," a type of extreme "devotion" (Blair-Loy 2009) to work—and often to a specific job category—that curtails professional workers' perceptions of their own agency. This is a concept that is important for understanding not only why commuter marriages occur but the meaning behind the occupational moves of role-identified professionals more generally.

In sum, commuter spouses are at the crux of a fundamental conflict between traditional family structure, changing gender roles, and the structure and meaning of postindustrial professional work. Throughout the book I have drawn on and extended literature in these three areas, to illuminate not only the challenges these spouses face but also the increasing incompatibility of work and family domains for professionals.

"Why Can't the Jobs Just Change?" Implications for Policy and Practice

My daughter, now four, is having a playdate at another child's house. As the girls slurp hot chocolate with rainbow marshmallows, I chat with the parents, whom I've only met recently. We get on the topic of my research, and I learn that they lived apart for a year of their marriage, while they were both finishing graduate school. We talk about Skype and texting and email, and how they never would have been in a commuter marriage if they'd had children at the time—though they recognized that, of course, some people do. It was interesting, the father said, how people changed their family lives to accommodate jobs, and how technology enabled them to do that. But "why can't the jobs just change?" he mused aloud.

On one hand, a potential answer to the father's question is that jobs have changed in some ways. There is a large literature about how the structure of contemporary employment has adapted to accommodate new configurations of work and family. Much research has explored organization-level changes in jobs, such as flextime (e.g., Hochschild 1997) and telecommuting (e.g., Gajendran and Harrison 2007). On the other hand, not all companies have permanently embraced such changes. In 2013, for example, Yahoo CEO Marissa Mayer terminated her company's popular work-from-home policy (Tkaczyk 2013). IBM ended the same benefit for many of its employees in 2017; before then, "about 40% of its nearly 400,000 employees worldwide did not have a traditional office" (Isidore 2017). Researchers have also pointed out that the United States lacks provisions at the federal level, such as paid maternity leave and universal childcare, that help families in many other industrialized nations to reconcile the demands of paid work and family (e.g., Coontz 2005). While commuter spouses may be a specific case, they reveal larger issues with the disjuncture between work and family in twenty-first-century America.

In this book, I have focused largely on the transformations that spouses and their children have made to their domestic lives in response to shifting social conditions. I have not discussed how jobs might change to better accommodate dual-career professional couples, so that these families might avoid being squeezed into configurations that they deem less than desirable. Yet my findings do suggest some key avenues for potential change on the work side of the work/family dichotomy.

First, on the employer side, organizations might consider changes that would enable them to retain workers who have family constraints, geographic or otherwise. These modifications may include the availability of flextime or telecommuting positions, as discussed above. As the differences between my study and research from the 1980s suggest, technology can be crucial to integrating paid work and family life. On one hand, we should be cautious about interpreting telecommuting as a panacea for all that ails professional workers. Clearly, it may not be feasible for every category of worker, or ideal for every individual worker's personality, to perform his or her functions remotely. On the other hand, decisions about the availability of remote work should be evidence based, rather than relying on a sense of what work is "supposed to" look like, and how workplaces have "always" been structured. For instance, one metaanalysis of 46 studies (Gajendran and Harrison 2007) found that telecommuting provided overall benefits to employers and employees, including increased job satisfaction, better performance, lower turnover, and decreased role stress, though "high-intensity" telecommuting (upwards of 2.5 days a week) had a deleterious effect on relations with coworkers.

Additionally, in cases where remote employment is not a possibility, organizations might consider other changes that could benefit their employees as well as themselves. Spousal and partner hiring is one such practice in academia, for instance. While controversial (D. Bell 2010) and also not a panacea, these hires are one mechanism for colleges and universities to attract and retain faculty members who are part of dual-career academic couples. Moreover, concerns about sacrificing the quality of applicants in these cases may be unfounded. One study found that academics who were hired as part of a couple outperformed their non-couple-hire colleagues, both in quantity of publications and in grant procurement (Woolstenhulme et al. 2012).

In addition to these implications for institutional practice, my findings also suggest the importance of making a broader shift in our cultural understanding of what it means to be successful in professional work. Commuter spouses are an extreme example of how the increased specialization of higher education and professional labor markets often means workers with advanced degrees are trained to think narrowly about the applicability of their skills. In a previous study (Lindemann, Tepper, and Talley 2017), my colleagues and I made this same argument about graduates of art programs, a large portion of whom go on to work in careers outside of the arts. To return to my own experience, I was trained in my graduate school to desire and seek a tenure-track academic job. That is indeed where I ended up, and I am content in that job, but my training in research might have been applicable to a variety of nonacademic organizations as well. Indeed, some of my peers are now happily and productively employed in other fields after prolonged academic job searches. Similarly, in the arts alumni study, while nearly 40 percent of employed arts graduates ended up working primarily in occupations unrelated to the arts (Lindemann and Tepper 2012), many of those graduates still found the skills they learned in arts school relevant to that non–arts work (Lindemann, Tepper, and Talley 2017). Conversely, some arts graduates are unhappily working in arts jobs, and some of my peers have clutched the brass ring of an academic position only to discard it upon finding themselves miserable. For these reasons, while it may seem counterintuitive as graduate and professional schools exist for increasingly specialized purposes, the burden is on those in higher education (including me) to ensure that our graduates have broad senses of their professional capabilities. Graduates should be emboldened to carve out different paths for themselves while still being viewed, and viewing themselves, as success stories. In sum, commuter spouses show us that the way that we train and professionalize students should acknowledge the tension between specialized training, the current availability of work, and the existence of family constraints.

I am aware that, in making these recommendations, I am framing commuter marriage as a problem to be solved. Some might rightly contend that the structure of the family has always been historically and culturally contingent, and they might argue that perhaps commuter marriage is simply another iteration of a form we falsely believe to be static. I would agree with this. Others might argue that individuals should be able to structure their family lives in whatever ways best align with their personal needs and predilections. While I agree with this point in theory, this is not what commuter spouses are doing. I do not view these arrangements as potentially problematic because they challenge normative conceptions of the family. I also do not view them as problematic for the same reasons as these couples' friends, extended family, and colleagues seem to—for instance, that these arrangements are a step toward divorce or are harmful for children. I have no evidence, based on my research, that any of those claims are either true or false. Instead, I view commuter marriages as potentially problematic largely because the people in them view them as problematic. Further, as I have argued, these spouses' sense of relative powerlessness over their arrangements exposes a fundamental incompatibility between domestic and occupational spheres today, particularly in the United States.

Another potentially problematic aspect of commuter marriage is that it may, paradoxically, contribute to gender inequality. This claim may seem counterintuitive, as these are ostensibly "egalitarian" marriages, in which both partners' careers are valued. Indeed, as discussed, women do seem to reap some disproportionate benefits from these arrangements. At the same time, they also seem to be disadvantaged in some ways. One hallmark of the literature on "(un)doing gender" is that gendered performances are not isolated acts that occur without context but that they either reaffirm or destabilize the gender-power structure. The fact that in the vast majority of commuter families with children, it was women not men who were doing the "single parenting" has important implications. As discussed in chapter 4, for example, studies of the motherhood penalty and fatherhood premium have suggested that the mechanisms between these unequal dynamics partially lie in the uneven gendered distribution of caretaking work (e.g., Avellar and Smock 2003; Budig and England 2001; Benard, Paik, and Correll 2007; Lundberg and Rose 2000; Waldfogel 1997).

Furthermore, my finding regarding "single parenthood" also resonates with a broader conversation about the relationship between feminist objectives and ongoing changes in the structure and meaning of marriage. Cancian (1990) has observed that a feminist ideological construct and an individualistic ideological construct are not necessarily one and the same; in fact, "The ideal of independence often leads to the reality of isolated individuals and impoverished mother-child households" (152). For most mothers in commuting relationships, their highly individualistic arrangements do not entail a gender-egalitarian division of parenting duties. If anything, these relationships place a greater burden on them as caretakers. In supporting Cancian's broader point that a heightened emphasis on individual fulfillment does not necessarily coincide with gender parity in the domestic sphere, my research provides an important coda to this broader literature.

What Doesn't This Book Say?

While this book has shined a light on various facets of commuter marriage, there remains some research to be done on these couples. One key area that might benefit from further illumination is the experiences of the children in these families. While I have explored parents' thoughts about their children, I did not interview any children of commuter spouses for the book, as my primary focus here was on the adults in the marriage. The psychological repercussions (if any) of commuter marriage on children is not something I can address, given my training and my data, but it is, I believe, an important question, particularly given the concerns of some of the parents I interviewed.

A second worthwhile avenue for further research would be to focus on same-sex commuter spouses. As discussed, I not able to locate any same-sex commuter couples to include in this study, partially because the project focused on marriage, and same-sex couples have until very recently been legally excluded from that institution. It would be worthwhile to incorporate data on same-sex commuter spouses, not only because the present study regrettably leaves out a subset of the population but also because previous research suggests that phenomena such as the wage penalty for motherhood may manifest differently in same-sex couples (e.g., Baumle 2009).

There are a variety of additional areas that I was unable to flesh out further in the book, given my scope and my interview questions, but that would benefit from further study. For instance, I have identified some types of gendered dynamics in these relationships—surrounding leisure time, perceived work productivity, and childcare roles. However, I have left question marks about others. Some of my data, for example, hint that these relationships may be associated with negative health outcomes, which may disproportionately impact men. In general, the health repercussions of these relationships should be more extensively studied. Future scholarship might also continue to trace the impacts of new technologies on the dynamics of these relationships.

Finally, my research here suggests that it is important to study not only commuter couples or LATs more generally, but also other types of families that are reimagining and reconfiguring their work and domestic lives in myriad ways. My findings about the entrenchment of professional role identities, for example, has relevance beyond commuter spouses. Future research should focus on the family decisions of professionals more broadly, evaluating the extent to which entrenchment in professional role identity predicts noncohabitation, "trailing," and "opting out" (P. Stone 2007) of the labor force. Research should also attend more closely to the school-to-career pipeline and trace the processes by which these identities get crystallized.

Final Thoughts

It is my sincere hope that this book proves useful and illuminating to those who find themselves in commuter marriages. As discussed in the prior chapter, many of my respondents expressed a desire to see the results of the study, in order to better understand their own experiences as part of something larger. Ideally these findings will resonate with them, and with other kinds of couples who lack time to spend together—for instance, spouses who live together but work opposite shifts—as well as with other individuals who are connecting the two pieces of the work/family puzzle in creative arrangements.

While this book is about one particular type of nonnormative marital arrangement, it extends our knowledge of the social forces that have brought this arrangement into being. The ways in which commuters talk about how others—and they, themselves—conceptualize their relationships reflect the durability of some cultural ideals surrounding marriage, despite how the institution has changed. Their gender roles hint at the possibility of a more egalitarian future, while bearing the imprint of the past. Their perceived lack of control over their lifestyle illuminates larger shifts in professional labor markets and the tenacity of role-identity.

This book, in sum, has not just been about commuter spouses, but about a series of changes that have impacted how many of us live and work in the twenty-first century. Born out of a specific convergence of historical circumstances, commuters represent a small fraction of all married people and all professional workers. Yet the narratives that these individuals tell about their relationships provide us with valuable insight into our own experiences as we fling our feet across the landscape of contemporary America, finding love, work, companionship, and—perhaps, if we are lucky—fulfillment.

Appendix A

METHODOLOGICAL APPENDIX

Data Collection

Data for this project were drawn from ninety-seven in-depth, semistructured interviews with individuals who had participated in commuter marriages. The sample included respondents who, at the time of their interviews, were in commuter arrangements, as well as those who had been part of such arrangements in the past.

I carried out the interviews between 2012 and 2013, primarily by phone, although six took place in person. Both phone and in-person interviews have their relative strengths and weaknesses (for an excellent summary, see Shuy 2003); however, due to respondents' geographic dispersal and my own limited resources, in most cases it was not feasible for me to sit down with respondents in person. While meeting with respondents may have helped me to build stronger rapports, I found nearly no differences between phone and in-person interviews in terms of the data gathered. The one distinction was that in-person interviews tended to yield

more analytic "noise"—that is, information that did not get coded because it was unconnected to the main themes of the study. For instance,
a discussion of places to eat in New York City ran for several pages of
one in-person interview transcript. Following Agar's (1996) assertion
that, in qualitative research, it is beneficial—and, at times, preferable—to
challenge one's respondents, I regularly asked follow-up questions and
engaged in pointed inquiry in order to encourage truthful and thorough
responses.

Interview topics included marital history, current marital dynamics and
satisfaction, occupational dimensions and satisfaction, communication
and use of technology, division of household labor and use of household
space, and future plans, as well as demographic questions. (For the interview schedule, see appendix B.) Interviews lasted, on average, about an
hour, with durations ranging from thirty-four minutes to over two hours.
I interviewed all respondents separately. Afterwards, I gave participants
the link to an online survey instrument, which included additional questions about potentially sensitive topics such as finances, sex, and emotional well-being. Eighty-eight respondents (91% of sample) filled out the
online questionnaire.

Sampling

Because of the overarching themes of this study—marriage, individualization, and the meaning of professional work—I focused on recruiting relatively well-educated, dual-earning married professionals who live(d) apart
due to their careers. This sampling strategy was consistent with purposive
sampling—or Glaser and Strauss's (1967) "theoretical sampling"—in that
I initially chose nodes with the aim of recruiting respondents with at least
a college education who were working in an array of professional careers.
I located participants through four nodes that selected on level of education as a proxy for professional work, as well as by snowball sampling
from each node: a university alumni email discussion list (n=28; 28.9%);
a professional email discussion list for academics (n=47; 48.5%); an email
discussion list for individuals in the Foreign Service (n=6; 6.2%); and my
own second-degree or third-degree contacts (n=16; 16.5%).

The discussion list appeals were made en masse to all members via introductory emails that specified the topic of the project and provided a link to the study website, as well as including a short statement about anonymity and voluntary consent. I recruited personal contacts through informal conversations as well as a post on social media. Across all of these nodes, the call for participants was sent to thousands of people.

Eligibility

Individuals were eligible to participate in the study if they were married and lived apart, or had done so in the past, for work-related reasons and maintained a separate residence for that purpose. I excluded unmarried couples because a major investigative aim of the overarching project was the evolving cultural construction of the institution of marriage. I used additional residence as a primary criterion for inclusion in the sample (as did Gerstel and Gross in their 1984 study) to avoid making evaluative and ultimately arbitrary distinctions between those who "traveled for work" and those who truly "lived apart."

Due to the well-documented additional relationship complications arising from deployment (e.g., Allen et al. 2010; Gambardella 2008; Newby et al. 2005), deployed military personnel were ineligible for the study. However, four respondents were members of the military currently living on bases in the United States, and I interviewed two of their partners as well.

I always sought to interview both spouses in a relationship, but this was not a necessary criterion for inclusion in the study. At the conclusion of each interview, I asked respondents whose spouses had not already participated if they would be willing to supply their partners' contact information; I then followed up with the partners. Fifty-six (57.7%) of the respondents were married to other people in the sample. It would have been preferable to have access to data from both halves of every couple, but it was not crucial, for a few reasons. First, while having the ability to interview both spouses in each couple would have been ideal for purposes of corroboration, it also did not make methodological sense to routinely exclude potential data on the basis of a spouse's unwillingness or inability to participate in the project. Second, because I focus on themes such as identity that apply to the individual, throughout the book I largely use the individual, rather than the couple, as the unit of analysis. Finally, as Gerstel and Gross (1984) point out, the concept that two spouses "constitute a single entity" (3) is in many ways problematic, and it is exactly this concept that commuter spouses are pushing against by living apart in service to their personal career goals. In my analysis, therefore, I find it appropriate to treat them as discrete individuals.[1] However, when possible, I do focus on cases in which I am able to incorporate the perspectives of both partners, as well as discussing instances in which respondents within the same couple interpreted their circumstances differently.

There was no minimum amount of time couples needed to have lived apart to qualify for the study. The amount of time spouses had spent living apart ranged from two months to sixteen years, with the median being about five years.[2] Similarly, there was no minimum duration of commute. In one instance, the two halves of the couple both commuted one hour to a midpoint house. Several other couples lived on separate continents with nearly a day's travel between them. The median total travel time between residences was about three and a half hours.

Though the eligibility criteria I used are different from those that other scholars have used, in many respects our samples are quite similar. For instance, most of Gerstel and Gross's respondents were in professional careers (1984, 207). Gerstel and Gross also limited their sample to spouses who spent a least three nights per week in their separate residences (1). While that was not an explicit criterion for eligibility in this project, nearly all of my respondents fit that category.

Sample Characteristics

All participants in the study had completed at least some college, and 70.5 percent had received graduate degrees. The majority of respondents—92.8 percent (89)—self-identified as white or Caucasian, whereas 4.1 percent (4) identified as Asian, 2.1 percent (2) identified as black, and 2.1 percent (2) identified as Hispanic or Latino. Zero identified with more than one race. In terms of income, 81.5 percent had individually earned $50,000 or more in the previous year. Their average age was 44.5, and their average age when they began living apart from their partners was 40.0. Sixty of the respondents (61.9%) were female, while thirty-seven (38.1%) were male. The median amount of time couples had spent living apart at their time of interview was about five years.

Thirty-six respondents (37.1%) had children under the age of 18 during the time they lived apart from their spouses; in all but three of these instances, women were the primary caregivers. At the time they began commuting, nine of these thirty-six had children aged five or younger, three had children aged six to twelve, fifteen had teenagers (aged thirteen to seventeen), and nine had children in more than one of these age categories. All children of respondents had one home in which they resided, rather than moving from one parent to another—except, in some cases, for visits.

The pathways by which couples entered into these commuting relationships were varied. Across the sixty-nine couples involved in this study (twenty-eight couples interviewed, plus forty-one individuals in additional couples), a majority (n=49; 71.0%) were in "satellite" relationships, where one partner remained in the family home they had previously shared while the other moved for a job opportunity. In about two thirds (n=33; 67.3%) of these satellite couples, the woman was the one remaining in the family home. In a minority of couples (n=16; 21.7%;), both partners had moved out of a shared home to pursue separate career ambitions in two different geographic regions. Finally, four couples (5.8% of couples) had never coresided. At the time of their interviews, none of the respondents were divorced from their noncohabitating partners.

Although, for ease of prose, I use the term "noncohabitating" to discuss these couples, in actuality all of the people in the sample lived with, or visited, their spouses at least some of the time. More than half (n=52; 53.6%) saw their spouses at least once a week, whereas 13.4 percent (n=13) reunited once at least every other week and 33.0 percent (n=32) saw them less than every two weeks. Across all ninety-seven respondents, 50.5 percent (n=49) said that the man did the bulk of the traveling, 26.8 percent (n=26) indicated that the woman traveled more of the time, and 22.6 percent (n=22) said that travel was more or less evenly split. In satellite relationships, the partner who had moved tended to do the bulk of the traveling back and forth to the family home. This was always the case when the satellite couple had children.

Many respondents' primary residences were located in the Southeast (n=36; 37.1%) or in the Mid Atlantic or New England regions (n=32; 32.0%) of the United States. Fewer were located in the plains or Great Lakes regions (n=10; 10.3%), the Far West (n=8; 8.2%), the Rocky Mountain or Southwest regions (n=3; 3.1%), or in other U.S. regions (n=1; 1.0%). Seven respondents (7.2%) resided primarily outside of the United States.

Academics in the Sample

Despite the use of multiple nodes intended to include various types of professional workers, respondents employed in higher education comprised over one-third (35.0%) of the sample. (As noted, 48.5% were recruited through a professional email discussion list for academics and snowballing from that node, but some of their spouses and referrals were nonacademics.) Since the characteristics of the U.S. commuter spouse population are not directly attainable with any demographic instruments that currently exist (Rindfuss and Stephen 1990, 261),[3] it is not possible to say with certainty whether people in higher education are "oversampled" in this study. I suspect that they are, though it is unclear to what extent.

Previous studies of long-distance relationships have also contained relatively high numbers of respondents employed in higher education. For instance, Mary Holmes (2014) focused solely on academics (see also Ferber and Loeb 1997), and about half of Gerstel and Gross's (1984) commuter sample consisted of academics. As the latter authors pointed out, while the relatively large number of academics may represent issues of sampling, it may also represent "the actual commuting population" (207), as academia lends itself to this lifestyle. Indeed, prior scholarship indicates that geographic separation is a particular concern for academic couples (Bruce 1990; Ferber and Loeb 1997; Wolf-Wendel, Twombly, and Rice 2000; Zippel 2017) and suggests that academics do tend to live apart from their partners at rates exceeding those of the general population (McFall and Murray-Close 2016). Additionally, it is important to emphasize that, while a large portion of respondents in this study were academics, they were not the majority of respondents. The project sheds light on commuter couples more broadly.

Data Analysis

Interview responses were audio recorded, transcribed, and hand coded. Relying on an inductive approach similar to "grounded-theory" (Glaser and Strauss 1967), I systematically examined the interview transcripts, sorting the data into units based on salient themes. I used orienting and analytic codes to group and compare units. I compared these findings across axes of difference, including age, gender, parental status, job field, type of residence, frequency of visitation, distance apart (in travel time), length of marriage, and length of time spent living apart.

All names of participants used in this book are pseudonyms. All potentially identifying information has been redacted or altered slightly for the purpose of maintaining anonymity.

Appendix B

INTERVIEW SCHEDULE

First, thank you very much for taking the time out to talk to me about your experience of living apart from your spouse. You have already signed a consent form, but I'd also like to get your verbal consent to be interviewed and taped. Do you consent?

First I'd like to ask you a little bit about yourself, if that's all right.

Prescreening Questions

Do you and your spouse both work full-time?

Do you live apart from your spouse, some or all of the time, due to the demands of your jobs?

Do you and your spouse have more than one residence (home or apartment) *because* of the demands of your jobs?

Could you have answered YES to all of the three questions above at some other point in your life? (They aren't true now, but they were true at one time.)

If ineligible: Unfortunately, you're not eligible for this study. I very much appreciate your taking the time out to talk to me today.
If eligible. . .

Demographics

I'd like to get a little bit of information about you to begin with, if that's okay.

How old are you?

What would you say is your race or ethnicity?

What do you do for work? (*Or:* What did you do for work when you lived apart from your spouse? Hereafter, tense changes are implied for couples who no longer live apart.)

What does your spouse do for work?

What is your spouse's gender?

Do you have any children? (*If yes:* Ages?)

Marital History

Great, now I'd like to get a little bit of information about your relationship with your spouse.

How did the two of you meet?

What first attracted you to your partner?

At the time you got married, what were your reasons for getting married?

Did you always know you wanted to get married?

How long have you been married to your partner?

When you first got married, did you live together for any period of time before living apart? (*If yes:* How long?)

If living together at some point: When you first moved in together, how did you set up a space together? How did you decide whose furniture to include in the house or apartment? Did you buy new furniture?

If living together at some point: When you lived together, how did you divide up the household labor? (Prompts: cooking, cleaning, childcare (if applicable))

Current Marital Situation

Could you briefly describe your current living situation with your partner? (Prompt questions: How often do you live apart and how often do you live together? What is the schedule like? Where do you live when you live apart, and where do you live when you live together?)

How far away from each other do you live when you live apart?

How did you come to have this relationship where you live apart? (Why do you do it?)

Whose decision was it to start living apart?

How long has this particular arrangement been going on?

Would you say that you are living apart because of financial necessity? Could you please explain?

Do you find that you have people in your life who challenge the fact that you live apart from your spouse? (*If yes:* Who are they? What do they say? How do you deal with it?)

Are there people who envy or admire your arrangement?

Occupational Dimensions and Satisfaction

What are the reasons why you work?

Do you like your current job? What do you/don't you like about it? Is this what you want to be doing for work in the long run?

Communicating and Technology

When you're living apart, how often would you say you're in communication with your partner over the phone? . . . In some way?

I'm going to list some forms of communication, and I'd like you to tell me what role they play in your relationship when you're living apart from your partner. For instance, how often you communicate this way, how important you feel it is to your relationship, and any other details you'd like to share:

Talking on the phone
Video chat (like Skype)

Online chatting, like IM or Gchat
Text messaging
Communicating through social networking sites, like posting on each
other's Facebook walls
Writing letters ("snail mail")

What would you say is the most important form of communication
through which you stay in touch with your partner when you're apart?
Do you and your partner visit each other when you're living apart?
(How often? Who visits whom? Is visiting important to you? If yes: Why?)

Maintaining Separate and Collective Spaces

In what ways would you say that you and your spouse rely on each other?
Could you talk a little bit about how you and your spouse divide up
household chores, like cooking, cleaning, laundry, and running errands?
(How about at the other residence?)
How do you think of your two residences? (Is one "yours" and one
your partner's? Are they both "both of yours"? Do you think of one as
more your home than the other?)
Who decorated each of the places?
How much control do you feel you have over your partner's space?
(*If children*) How do you divide up childcare?
Could you tell me about the last argument you had with your partner
while you were apart? What was it about? How did you resolve it?

Attitudes about Marriage/Satisfaction

Only answer this if you feel comfortable, but would you say that you're
satisfied with your marriage? Please explain. (What are you satisfied with
and/or not satisfied with?)
What would you say you like the *most* about being married?
Do you think it's important for people, in general, to get married?
Please explain.
Would you agree with the statement "Marriage is sacred"? (Why?/
Why not?)

Looking to the Future

Do you think at some point you will start living with your spouse permanently again?

If end is anticipated: Is there a time clock on it ("We'll do this for two more years") or do you think there is something that needs to happen in your lives that would cause you to live together permanently again?

If past tense: Why did you stop living apart from your spouse? Whose decision was it to stop living apart?

Miscellaneous

What, if anything, do you like *least* about living apart from your spouse?

What, if anything, do you like *most* about living apart from your spouse?

Do you have any advice for other couples who are thinking about living apart?

Is there anything else you think I should know about your experience of being in a marriage where you don't live together all of the time?

Do you think your spouse would be willing to be interviewed by me [*if not interviewed yet*]? [*If yes, get contact information.*]

Just one more thing: I would be very grateful if you would fill out a short survey so that I can get some more information. Your answers to this survey will never be connected to your responses to the interview questions, so I will never know what your particular answers were. [*Include information about how to access online survey.*]

Thanks so much for taking the time out to talk to me. If you think of anything else you want to tell me, or if you have any questions or concerns, you have my contact information.

Appendix C

Follow-up Survey

1. What is the highest level of school that you have completed?
   Less than high school
   Some high school
   High school diploma or GED
   Some college
   Undergraduate degree
   Some graduate school
   Graduate degree

2. What is the highest level of school YOUR SPOUSE has completed?
   Less than high school
   Some high school
   High school diploma or GED
   Some college
   Undergraduate degree
   Some graduate school
   Graduate degree

3. How would you describe yourself politically?
   Liberal
   Conservative
   Moderate
   Depends on the issue
   I am not political
   Other (please explain)

4. What was the COMBINED annual income last year of you and your spouse?
   $100,000 or less
   $100,001 to $150,000
   $150,001 to $250,000
   $250,001 to $350,000
   $350,001 to $450,000
   More than $450,000

5. What was your INDIVIDUAL income last year?
   $10,000 or less
   $10,001 to $20,000
   $30,001 to $40,000
   $40,001 to $50,000
   $50,001 to $60,000
   $60,001 to $70,000
   $70,001 to $80,000
   $80,001 to $90,000
   $90,001 to $100,000
   $100,001 to $150,000
   More than $150,000

6. Family (including your spouse) is . . .
   . . . the most important element in your life.
   . . . an important element in your life, but not THE most important.
   . . . not an important element in your life.

7. How satisfied are you with your family life (including your marriage)?
   I am very satisfied with my family life
   I am somewhat satisfied with my family life
   I am somewhat dissatisfied with my family life
   I am very dissatisfied with my family life
   Unsure

8. Would you say that you and your spouse have a closer relationship than your parents had/have with each other?

> My spouse and I have a closer relationship than my parents had/have with each other
>
> My spouse and I have the same level of closeness that my parents had/have with each other
>
> My parents had/have a closer relationship than my spouse and I have
>
> Unsure

9. How many times did you and your spouse have sex in the average month, while you were living apart? (Please write in a number).

10. How would you rate your level of satisfaction with your sex life while you were living apart?

> Not at all satisfied
>
> Somewhat satisfied
>
> Moderately satisfied
>
> Extremely satisfied
>
> Not sure

NOTES

Introduction

1. While the percentage of all married couples in the United States who do not cohabitate due to their jobs is not directly measurable, empirical data demonstrate that the lifestyle is on the rise in a number of European countries and Canada. David Popenoe, the codirector of the National Marriage Project at Rutgers University, told the *New York Times* that from "partly what we know anecdotally, partly the fact that every other significant European trend in family life has turned out to be happening in America" it is clear that the number of commuter spouses stateside is increasing as well (Brooke 2006).

2. "Over the past forty years, the proportion of the academic labor force holding full-time tenured positions has declined by 26 percent and the share holding full-time tenure-track positions has declined by an astonishing 50 percent," the American Association of University Professors found. "Conversely, there has been a 62 percent increase in full-time non-tenure-track faculty appointments and a 70 percent increase in part-time instructional faculty appointments" (2016, 13).

3. Rindfuss and Stephen (1990, 259) found that the most common reasons for spouses to live apart were military service and incarceration and that different reasons for living separately involved different challenges and had varying outcomes.

4. For instance, most of the respondents in Gerstel and Gross's 1984 book *Commuter Marriage: A Study of Work and Family* were in professional careers (207). The authors indicate that "among commuters—by definition dual-career families—it is the presence of two careers pursued simultaneously rather than the nature of any single job which requires that couples live apart" (6).

5. Murray-Close used the 5-percent sample of the 2000 United States Census, including respondents between the ages of 25 and 54, who had a college degree or more, who reported that they were "married" but not "separated," who worked for pay in a civilian occupation for the past five years, and who resided in a household (versus group quarters) (2013, 5). It is important to note that these estimates would be higher if expanded to include unmarried couples. By one calculation, for instance, 9% of adults in Britain are in relationships but not living with their partners (Duncan et al. 2013).

6. Its focus on the professional class also distinguishes this book from some prior scholarship. In her 1985 book on commuter marriages, Winfield argued that there was "no particular need to distinguish between middle-class and working-class commuter marriages" because "the problems and pleasures are much the same" (xvi). Yet Winfield's research questions were different from mine. While I, too, touch on the "problems and pleasures" that these couples experience, one of my central concerns is how the structure and meaning of professional work, in combination with the trend toward individualization, contribute to these arrangements.

1. Apart Together

1. This orientation toward marriage is now evident in a variety of broad attitudinal shifts reflecting the value placed on individual autonomy and the increasing tolerance of a diversity of relationship behaviors such as divorce, choosing to remain childless (Thornton and Young DeMarco 2001), and same-sex marriage (Avery et al. 2007). And as historian Stephanie Coontz (2005) points out, the dearth of family-friendly social policies (e.g., subsidized parental leave, flexible work schedules, and affordable childcare) in the United States plays into this concept of individualization (313).

2. Research based on Giddens's premise has been scant and leaves much room for further investigation. Hall (1996) and Gross and Simmons (2002) have been notable in their efforts to integrate data and the "pure relationship" frame. Hall, using data from the Canadian Fertility Survey, found that couples in "pure" relationships were more likely to divorce, and Gross and Simmons, based on a survey of middle-aged adults in the United States, found that those in "pure love" relationships reaped the benefits and experienced few of the negative side effects found by Giddens (Gross and Simmons 2002, 531).

3. Eighty-eight respondents received and replied to this question.

4. Some authors have previously applied the concept of "apart togetherness" to commuter spouses (e.g., Murray-Close 2013). In addition, a broader literature has focused on the "Living Apart Together" lifestyle—which includes both unmarried and married partners who do not cohabitate for a variety of reasons (e.g., Levin 2004; Levin and Trost 1999).

5. Gerstel and Gross (1984), too, observed that "heightened communication" was sometimes a benefit of these relationships (75)

6. Similarly, one respondent told Winfield (1985) that seeing her husband was akin to "a honeymoon every week" (xiv).

7. Seventy-four respondents answered the question.

8. This is based on an analysis of survey data from the National Opinion Research Center, looking at the average frequency of sex for sexually active, married respondents under age sixty.

9. Eighty-four respondents answered the question. Respondents who had resumed cohabitating were asked to reflect on the period during which they had lived apart.

10. As I discuss in chapter 6, one couple had gotten divorced and then remarried each other.

11. In fact, Bergen (2010a) found that commuter wives justified their arrangements by emphasizing the similarities of their marriages to the dominant U.S. "master narrative" about marriage (47).

12. Indeed, speech communication scholar Andrea Towers Scott (2002) has observed that "shared tasks as a relationship sustenance strategy successfully predicted feelings of connection" within long-distance marriages (viii).

13. Further, these responses bolster evidence from prior studies suggesting that symbolic significance becomes an important feature of long-distance relationships. Winfield (1985), for instance, cited commitment to the relationship as the reason commuter couples show a higher rate of fidelity, suggesting that this statistic demonstrated their valuing of the marital bond. Gerstel and Gross (1982) observed that commuter spouses cling to these relationships, rather than disengaging from them, which indicates that they positively value the bond. And a related study found that college students in long-distance relationships were "more in love" and tended to idealize their relationships more than geographically close couples (Stafford and Reske 1990, 274).

14. Other response options were "My spouse and I have the same level of closeness that my parents had/have with each other" and "My parents had/have a closer relationship than my spouse and I have." This question was part of my follow-up survey.

15. Other response options were "an important element in your life, but not *the* most important" and "not an important element in your life." This question was part of my follow-up survey.

16. Gerstel and Gross (1984), too, pointed out that, in many of their characteristics, including "the maintenance of bonds between husband and wife and parents and children, as well as the striving for success in the work world," commuter spouses reflected "the mainstream of American values" (2).

17. Mary Holmes (2004a) phrased this more eloquently than I do, in her research on academic couples in the United Kingdom who live apart: "Distance does not always bring intimacy to an end. Distance relationships perhaps merely highlight a paradox within all relationships: yearning to be close though distant, separate though together" (186).

2. Virtually Together

1. This finding is in line with prior research demonstrating how long-distance couples, such as dating college students, "use video to 'hang out' together and engage in activities over extended periods of time" (Neustaedter and Greenberg 2012, 753).

2. Mary Holmes (2014), too, explores the concept of "home" in her work on couples who live apart.

3. This was across the eighty-nine respondents whom I asked about their frequency of communication while apart ("When you're living apart, how often would you say you're in communication with your partner in some way?").

4. Similarly, in her study of transnational families, Raelene Wilding (2006) has found that the introduction of email provided "a sense of transcending time and space, which contributes to a perception of intimate connectedness" (138).

5. However, it is still true that they cannot necessarily do it "jointly in an easy, spontaneous way," as was the case for Gerstel and Gross's respondents (1984, 61).

6. Interestingly, in the case of one couple, the wife said that the time apart had negatively impacted the quality of their communication, while her husband told me that their communication had improved.

7. Previous scholarship has also pinpointed other pitfalls of using emergent technologies to communicate and to mutually handle logistics. One study (Li 2007) found that small groups working together to solve problems via computers took twice as long as face-to-face groups to complete tasks—however, the computer-mediated group required less communication. Psychological research, furthermore, suggests that study participants feel a higher degree

of closeness when they speak in person, versus online (Mallen, Day, and Green 2003), and that communication via computer has other important social psychological repercussions that are distinct from those arising in face-to-face contact (Kiesler, Siegel, and McGuire 1984).

8. Three of my respondents (from three different couples) even said that having children was what kept their marriages together despite the geographic separation. One pointed out, for instance, that if it had not been for her child, "I probably would have just gotten fed up and said, 'Oh well, this isn't working out' and ended it."

9. This finding aligns with other work on long-distance partners. Sociologist Orsolya Kolozsvari (2015) has found, for instance, that these couples "created joint socio-mental spaces, which enhanced their sense of belonging and helped to expand definitions of intimacy and space" (302).

10. Prior research has also emphasized that one pitfall of nonverbal communication, such as email, is that it often lacks conversational clues, such as gestures, emphasis, and tone (Kruger et al. 2005).

11. Apparently, you should ask the redcap at the desk. He or she always knows in advance.

3. Nobody's Decision

1. Putatively, one of the initial goals of the sociology of deviance was to "study the processes by which people become labeled deviant, so as to reveal, by contrast, the ideological construction of 'the normal'" (Epstein 1994, 197). However, in practice, scholars of deviance have largely focused on liminal and marginalized populations, in and of themselves, without exploring what they could reveal about the topography of the broader social landscape.

2. "A family consists of a householder and one or more other people living in the same household who are related to the householder by birth, marriage or adoption" (Pemberton 2015).

3. While a majority of my respondents said that they had encountered stigma for their lifestyle, a substantial portion did not. This may be evidence of the realization of Winfield's prediction: that, indeed, this lifestyle has become more normalized. As discussed, academics in particular spoke to this normalization, at least among their colleagues, if not among others in their lives. But respondents in other fields also emphasized the prevalence of the arrangement. As one respondent, a CEO, told me: "I think working remotely and commuting and living in one place and working in another is a professional necessity now."

4. Winfield's (1985) respondents, too, indicated that family and friends thought their lifestyle was the final step before divorce.

5. Gerstel and Gross (1984) touched on this topic as well, finding similarly that the commuter spouses in their study "seem neither to have agonized over nor even to have seen their decisions as a matter of choice" (23).

6. Also, while Merton's original argument concentrated on material assets, he did not specify that the cultural goals in question must be strictly financial in nature. In fact, in his 1938 article, he pointed out that his formulation was "concerned primarily with economic activity in the broad sense" mainly because applying this formulation to "various spheres of conduct" would render the paper unwieldy (676).

7. Other researchers (for instance, Agnew et al. 1996) have also focused on the importance of relative, rather than absolute, deprivation.

8. Interestingly, "that their primary motivation for living apart is career-related but not primarily financial" (6) was one criterion for inclusion in Gerstel and Gross's 1984 study.

9. Ecklund, Park, and Veliz (2008), for example, have found that, for some, "being a scientist forms a sort of master identity over the identities of gender and race" (1827).

10. For instance, one commuter who worked for his state government indicated that although the first time he lived apart from his wife was not due to financial necessity, the next two times were. "I mean, we've had sustained periods of unemployment," he told me, "so that's depleted our financial resources."

11. They observed that "the existence of couples who independently pursue individual economic fortune suggests that this presumption of common economic fate and a common household can no longer meet the realities of an economy and a family which increasingly contains two earners" (9).

4. "They Don't Have to Pick up Their Husbands' Shoes"

1. This theoretical orientation is in line with Risman's (1998) description of the combined "gender structure" and "doing gender" approach.

2. Commuters' divergence from the model of the trailing spouse has caused Winfield (1985) to interpret the commuter marriage as a "female-determined relationship" (4). And Van der Klis and Mulder (2008) have found that gender ideology is associated with the choice to enter into a commuter partnership.

3. Mary Holmes's work on long-distance relationships among academics, for instance, suggests that women are judged more harshly than their male partners when they prioritize their careers and enter into these arrangements (2004b, 2014) and that women in these nontraditional relationships often remain in caretaking roles (2004a). Bergen, Kirby, and McBride (2007), too, found that commuter wives often encountered "traditional gendered expectations for unpaid family labor" (287), and McBride and Bergen (2014) have observed that commuter wives' narratives about their marriages "had to respond to the large cultural discourse on marriage and motherhood (also buttressed by discourses of community and patriarchal discourses of the role of women)" (569). While these latter studies do not explicitly compare female to male commuter spouses, they suggest possible differences in the lived experiences of wives and husbands in these marriages.

4. There were no cases in which children traveled back and forth between husband and wife, as in some divorced families.

5. In addition, there were other respondents whose narratives did not conform to the general patterns discussed in this chapter. Some commuter spouses, both men and women, did not talk about their housework either increasing or decreasing during their time apart. And one male respondent, like many female respondents, explicitly drew a connection between living apart and a decrease in his share of household labor. He told me (and his wife agreed) that he had done the bulk of the cooking and cleaning when the couple lived together. Tellingly, this couple, like Ethan and Hannah, were reflective about the unusualness of their division of labor. The wife remarked, for instance, "We're weird like that."

6. Moreover, the persistence of normative gendered expectations among my respondents aligns with more recent work on commuter wives (e.g., Bergen, Kirby, and McBride 2007) as well as other types of noncohabitating couples (Levin 2004, 238).

5. Who Benefits from (Commuter) Marriage?

1. Young 2014.

2. Fifty-five female commuters and thirty-five male commuters responded to this question. Others responded that they did not know, or they did not receive this question.

6. "But Are They Happy?"

1. Interestingly, Gerstel and Gross (1984) reflected that they were often asked a related question: "Does commuter marriage work?" (14).

2. As Gerstel and Gross (1984) pointed out, "Changes in the commuters' marriages remind us that the constant presence of both spouses does not always lead to harmonious and relaxed interaction. Instead, it often leads to boredom and an intensification not a reduction of tension" (53).

3. Other research (e.g., Gerstel and Gross 1984; Gross 1980b; Winfield 1985) has discussed this theme as well.

Appendix A: Methodological Appendix

1. Winfield (1985), similarly, interviewed fifty-nine spouses in commuter marriages—only twelve of whom were married to each other (xvi).

2. This included noncontiguous stints living apart. For instance, a couple who had lived apart for three years, then together for two, then apart for three, was coded as living apart for six years.

3. Murray-Close (2013) estimates them indirectly with census data.

References

Acker, Joan. 1990. "Hierarchies, Jobs, Bodies: A Theory of Gendered Organizations." *Gender & Society* 4, no. 2: 139–58. https://doi.org/10.1177/089124390004002002.

Agar, Michael. 1996. *The Professional Stranger: An Informal Introduction to Ethnography*. San Diego, CA: Academic Press.

Agnew, Robert. 2005. *Pressured into Crime: An Overview of General Strain Theory*. Los Angeles, CA: Roxbury.

Agnew, Robert, Francis T. Cullen, Velmer S. Burton, Jr., T. David Evans, and R. Gregory Dunaway. 1996. "A New Test of Classic Strain Theory." *Justice Quarterly* 13, no. 4: 681–704. https://doi.org/10.1080/07418829600093151.

Akers, Ronald L., Marvin D. Krohn, Lonn Lanza-Kaduce, and Marcia Radosevich. 1979. "Social Learning and Deviant Behavior: A Specific Test of a General Theory." *American Sociological Review* 44, no. 4 (August): 636–55. www.jstor.org/stable/2094592.

Allen, Elizabeth S., Galena K. Rhoades, Scott M. Stanley, and Howard J. Markman. 2010. "Hitting Home: Relationships between Recent Deployment, Posttraumatic Stress Symptoms, and Marital Functioning for Army Couples." *Journal of Family Psychology* 24, no. 3 (June): 280–88. https://doi.org/10.1037/a0019405.

Amato, Paul R., David R. Johnson, Alan Booth, and Stacy J. Rogers. 2003. "Continuity and Change in Marital Quality between 1980 and 2000." *Journal of Marriage and Family* 65, no. 1 (February): 1–22. https://doi.org/10.1111/j.1741-3737.2003.00001.x.

Amato, Paul, Alan Booth, David Johnson, and Stacy Rogers. 2007. *Alone Together: How Marriage in America is Changing*. Cambridge, MA: Harvard University Press.

American Association of University Professors. 2016. "The Annual Report on the Economic Status of the Profession, 2015–16. Higher Education at a Crossroads: The Economic Value of Tenure and the Future of the Profession." *Academe* (March–April). https://www.aaup.org/sites/default/files/2015-16EconomicStatusReport.pdf.

Anderson, Deborah J., Melissa Binder, and Kate Krause. 2002. "The Motherhood Wage Penalty: Which Mothers Pay It and Why?" *The American Economic Review* 92, no. 2 (May): 354–58. http://www.jstor.org/stable/3083431.

Anderson, Elaine A., and Jane W. Spruill. 1993. "The Dual-Career Commuter Family: A Lifestyle on the Move." *Marriage & Family Review* 19, nos. 1–2: 131–47. https://doi.org/10.1300/J002v19n01_08.

Avellar, Sarah, and Pamela J. Smock. 2003. "Has the Price of Motherhood Declined over Time? A Cross-Cohort Comparison of the Motherhood Wage Penalty." *Journal of Marriage and Family* 65, no. 3 (August): 597–607. https://doi.org/10.1111/j.1741-3737.2003.00597.x.

Avery, Alison, Justin Chase, Linda Johansson, Samantha Litvak, Darrel Montero, and Michael Wydra. 2007. "America's Changing Attitudes toward Homosexuality, Civil Unions, and Same-Gender Marriage: 1977–2004." *Social Work* 52, no. 1 (January): 71–79. https://doi.org/10.1093/sw/52.1.71.

Bank, Barbara J., and Suzanne L. Hansford. 2000. "Gender and Friendship: Why Are Men's Best Same-Sex Friendships Less Intimate and Supportive?" *Personal Relationships* 7, no. 1 (March): 63–78. https://doi.org/10.1111/j.1475-6811.2000.tb00004.x.

Bauman, Zygmunt. 2003. *Liquid Love: On the Frailty of Human Bonds*. Malden, MA: Blackwell.

Baumle, Amanda K. 2009. "The Cost of Parenthood: Unraveling the Effects of Sexual Orientation and Gender on Income." *Social Science Quarterly* 90, no. 4 (December): 983–1002. https://doi.org/10.1111/j.1540-6237.2009.00673.x.

Bearce, M. 2013. *Super Commuter Couples: Staying Together When a Job Keeps You Apart*. Wayzata, MN: Equanimity Press.

Beck, Ulrich, and Elisabeth Beck-Gernsheim. 1995. *The Normal Chaos of Love*. Cambridge: Polity.

Beck, Ulrich, and Elisabeth Beck-Gernsheim. 2014. *Distant Love: Personal Life in the Global Age*. Translated by Rodney Livingstone. Malden, MA: Polity.

Beck-Gernsheim, Elisabeth. 2002. *Reinventing the Family: In Search of New Lifestyles*. Cambridge: Polity.

Becker, Penny Edgell, and Phyllis Moen. 1999. "Scaling Back: Dual-Earner Couples' Work-Family Strategies." *Journal of Marriage and the Family* 61, no. 4 (November): 995–1007. https://doi.org/10.2307/354019.

Bell, David A. 2010. "The Intricacies of Spousal Hiring." *Chronicle of Higher Education* 56. https://www.chronicle.com/article/The-Intricacies-of-Spousal/65456.

Bell, Robert R. 1981. *Worlds of Friendship*. Beverly Hills, CA: Sage.

Bellah, Robert N., Richard Madsen, William M. Sullivan, Ann Swidler, and Steven M. Tipton. 2007. *Habits of the Heart: Individualism and Commitment in American Life*. Berkeley: University of California Press.

Benard, Stephen, In Paik, and Shelley J. Correll. 2007. "Cognitive Bias and the Mother-hood Penalty." *Hastings Law Journal* 59, no. 6: 1359–87. http://heinonline.org/hol-cgi-bin/get_pdf.cgi?handle=hein.journals/hastlj59&section=49.

Bennett, Rosemary. 2007. "Couples That Live Apart . . . Stay Together." *Times,* May 12. https://www.thetimes.co.uk/article/couples-that-live-apart-stay-together-rx7bj7tnbkf.

Bergen, Karla Mason. 2010a. "Accounting for Difference: Commuter Wives and the Master Narrative of Marriage." *Journal of Applied Communication Research* 38, no. 1: 47–64. https://doi.org/10.1080/00909880903483565.

———. 2010b. "Negotiating a 'Questionable' Identity: Commuter Wives and Social Networks." *Southern Communication Journal* 75, no. 1: 35–56. https://doi.org/10.1080/10417940902951816.

———. 2014. "Discourse Dependence in the Commuter Family." In *Remaking "Family" Communicatively,* edited by Leslie A. Baxter, 211–28. New York: Peter Lang.

Bergen, Karla Mason, Erika Kirby, and M. Chad McBride. 2007. " 'How Do You Get Two Houses Cleaned?': Accomplishing Family Caregiving in Commuter Mar-riages." *Journal of Family Communication* 7, no. 4: 287–307. https://doi.org/10.1080/15267430701392131.

Berk, Sarah F. 1985. *The Gender Factory: The Apportionment of Work in American Households.* New York: Plenum.

Bianchi, Suzanne M., Melissa A. Milkie, Liana C. Sayer, and John P. Robinson. 2000. "Is Anyone Doing the Housework? Trends in the Gender Division of Household Labor." *Social Forces* 79, no. 1 (September): 191–228. https://doi.org/10.1093/sf/79.1.191.

Bielby, William T., and Denise D. Bielby. 1992. "I Will Follow Him: Family Ties, Gender-Role Beliefs, and Reluctance to Relocate for a Better Job." *American Journal of Sociology* 97, no. 5 (March): 1241–67. https://doi.org/10.1086/229901.

Binstock, Georgina, and Arland Thornton. 2003. "Separations, Reconciliations, and Living Apart in Cohabiting and Marital Unions." *Journal of Marriage and Family* 65, no. 2 (May): 432–43. https://doi.org/10.1111/j.1741-3737.2003.00432.x.

Bittman, Michael, and Judy Wajcman. 2000. "The Rush Hour: The Character of Lei-sure Time and Gender Equity." *Social Forces* 79, no. 1 (September): 165–89. https://doi.org/10.1093/sf/79.1.165.

Blair-Loy, Mary. 2009. *Competing Devotions: Career and Family among Women Exec-utives.* Cambridge, MA: Harvard University Press.

Bradburn, Norman M. 1969. *The Structure of Psychological Well-Being.* Chicago: Aldine.

Brines, Julie. 1994. "Economic Dependency, Gender, and the Division of Labor at Home." *American Journal of Sociology* 100, no. 3 (November): 652–88. https://doi.org10.1086/230577.

Brooke, Jill. 2006. "Home Alone Together." *New York Times,* May 4. http://www.nytimes.com/2006/05/04/garden/04lat.html.

Browne, Irene, and Joya Misra. 2003. "The Intersection of Gender and Race in the Labor Market." *Annual Review of Sociology* 29: 487–513. https://doi.org/10.1146/annurev.soc.29.010202.100016.

Bruce, Willa. 1990. "Dual-Career Couples in the University: Policies and Problems." Paper presented at the annual conference of the National Association for Women Deans, Administrators and Counselors, Nashville, Tennessee, March 21–25.

Budig, Michelle J., and Paula England. 2001. "The Wage Penalty for Motherhood." *American Sociological Review* 66, no. 2 (April): 204–25. http://www.jstor.org/stable/2657415.

Bunker, Barbara B., Josephine M. Zubek, Virginia J. Vanderslice, and Robert W. Rice. 1992. "Quality of Life in Dual-Career Families: Commuting Versus Single-Residence Couples." *Journal of Marriage and the Family* 54, no. 2 (May): 399–407. https://doi.org/10.2307/353071.

Butler, Judith. 2004. *Undoing Gender*. New York: Routledge.

Cain, Susan. 2013. *Quiet: The Power of Introverts in a World That Can't Stop Talking*. New York: Random House.

Cairncross, Frances. 1997. *The Death of Distance: How the Communications Revolution Will Change Our Lives*. Boston, MA: Harvard Business School Press.

Callero, Peter L. 1985. "Role-Identity Salience." *Social Psychology Quarterly* 48, no. 3: 203–15. http://www.jstor.org/stable/3033681.

Cancian, Francesca M. 1990. *Love in America: Gender and Self-Development*. New York: Cambridge University Press.

Capowich, George E., Paul Mazerolle, and Alex Piquero. 2001. "General Strain Theory, Situational Anger, and Social Networks: An Assessment of Conditioning Influences." *Journal of Criminal Justice* 29, no. 5: 445–61. httos://doi.org/10.1016/S0047-2352(01)00101-5.

Carter, Julia. 2012. "What Is Commitment? Women's Accounts of Intimate Attachment." *Families, Relationships and Societies* 1, no. 2 (June): 137–53. http://doi.org/10.1332/204674312X645484.

Cashion, Barbara G. 1970. "Durkheim's Concept of Anomie and its Relationship to Divorce." *Sociology and Social Research* 55, no. 1: 72–81.

Castles, Stephen, and Godula Kosack. 1973. *Immigrant Workers and Class Structure in Western Europe*. London: Oxford University Press.

Cherlin, Andrew J. 1992. *Marriage, Divorce, Remarriage*. Cambridge, MA: Harvard University Press.

———. 2004. "The Deinstitutionalization of American Marriage." *Journal of Marriage and Family* 66, no. 4 (November): 848–61. http://doi.org/10.1111/j.0022-2445.2004.00058.x.

———. 2009. *The Marriage-Go-Round: The State of Marriage and the Family in America Today*. New York: Knopf.

Clarke, Marie, Abbey Hyde, and Jonathan Drennan. 2013. "Professional Identity in Higher Education." In *The Academic Profession in Europe: New Tasks and New Challenges*, edited by Barbara M. Kehm and Ulrich Teichler, 7–22. New York: Springer.

Cleveland, Jeanette N., Gwenith G. Fisher, and Katina B. Sawyer. 2015. "Work—Life Equality: The Importance of a Level Playing Field at Home." In *Gender and the Work-Family Experience*, edited by Maura J. Mills, 177–99. New York: Springer.

Coe, Cati. 2011. "What Is Love? The Materiality of Care in Ghanaian Transnational Families." *International Migration* 49, no. 6 (December): 7–24. https://doi.org/10.1111/j.1468-2435.2011.00704.x.

Connell, Raewyn. 1987. *Gender and Power: Society, the Person and Sexual Politics*. Cambridge: Polity.

Coombs, Robert H. 1991. "Marital Status and Personal Well-Being: A Literature Review." *Family Relations* 40, no. 1: 97–102. https://doi.org/10.2307/585665.

Coontz, Stephanie. 2000. "Historical Perspectives on Family Studies." *Journal of Marriage and Family* 62, no. 2 (May): 283–97. https://doi.org/10.1111/j.1741-3737.2000. 00283.x.

——. 2005. *The Marriage, a History: From Obedience to Intimacy or How Love Conquered Marriage*. New York: Viking.

Deutsch, Francine M. 2007. "Undoing Gender." *Gender & Society* 21, no. 1: 106–27. https://doi.org/10.1177/0891243206293577

Dilworth, Jennie E. Long. 2004. "Predictors of Negative Spillover from Family to Work." *Journal of Family Issues* 25, no. 2: 241–61. https://doi.org/10.1177/ 0192513X03257406.

Dizard, Jan E., and Howard Gadlin. 1991. *The Minimal Family*. Amherst: University of Massachusetts Press.

Dubrovsky, Vitaly J., Sara Kiesler, and Beheruz N. Sethna. 1991. "The Equalization Phenomenon: Status Effects in Computer-Mediated and Face-to-Face Decision-Making Groups." *Human-Computer Interaction* 6, no. 2: 119–46. https://doi.org/10.1207/ s15327051hci0602_2.

Duncan, Simon, Miranda Phillips, Sasha Roseneil, Julia Carter, and Mariya Stoilova. 2013. "Living Apart Together: Uncoupling Intimacy and Co-Residence." Research Briefing. April 22. http://www.bbk.ac.uk/news/living-apart-together/LivingApart Together_MultiMethodAnalysis_BriefingPaper_22April2013.pdf

Durkheim, Emile. (1897) 1951. *Suicide: A Study in Sociology*. Translated by John A. Spaulding and George Simpson. Glencoe, IL: Free Press.

Ecklund, Elaine Howard, Jerry Z. Park, and Phil Todd Veliz. 2008. "Secularization and Religious Change among Elite Scientists." *Social Forces* 86, no. 4 (June): 1805–39. https://doi.org/10.1353/sof.0.0048.

Edin, Kathryn, and Maria Kefalas. 2011. *Promises I Can Keep: Why Poor Women Put Motherhood before Marriage*. Berkeley: University of California Press.

Edin, Kathryn, and Joanna M. Reed. 2005. "Why Don't They Just Get Married? Barriers to Marriage among the Disadvantaged." *The Future of Children* 15, no. 2 (Fall): 117–37. http://files.eric.ed.gov/fulltext/EJ795854.pdf.

Ellis, Carolyn. 2004. *The Ethnographic I: A Methodological Novel about Autoethnography*. New York: Rowman Altamira.

Epstein, Steven. 1994. "A Queer Encounter: Sociology and the Study of Sexuality." *Sociological Theory* 12, no. 2 (July): 188–202. https://doi.org/10.2307/201864.

Fehr, Beverley Anne. 1996. *Friendship Processes*. Thousand Oaks, CA: Sage.

Ferber, Marianne A., and Jane W. Loeb, eds. 1997. *Academic Couples: Problems and Promises*. Urbana: University of Illinois Press.

Gajendran, Ravi S., and David A. Harrison. 2007. "The Good, the Bad, and the Unknown about Telecommuting: Meta-analysis of Psychological Mediators and Individual Consequences." *Journal of Applied Psychology* 92, no. 6: 1524–41. https://doi. org/10.1037/0021-9010.92.6.1524.

Gambardella, Lucille C. 2008. "Role-Exit Theory and Marital Discord Following Extended Military Deployment." *Perspectives in Psychiatric Care* 44, no. 3 (July): 169–74. https://doi.org/10.1111/j.1744-6163.2008.00171.x.

Ganong, Lawrence H., Marilyn Coleman, Richard Feistman, Tyler Jamison, and Melinda Stafford Markham. 2012. "Communication Technology and Postdivorce Coparenting." *Family Relations* 61, no. 3 (July): 397–409. https://doi.org/10.1111/j.1741-3729.2012.00706.x.

Gassmann, Jaime Nicole Noble. 2010. "Patrolling the Homefront: The Emotional Labor of Army Wives Volunteering in Family Readiness Groups." PhD diss., University of Kansas.

Geertz, Clifford. 1994. "Thick Description: Toward an Interpretive Theory of Culture." In *Readings in the Philosophy of Social Science*, edited by Michael Martin and Lee C. McIntyre, 213–32. Cambridge, MA: MIT Press.

Gershuny, Jonathan. 2000. *Changing Times*. Oxford: Oxford University Press.

Gerson, Kathleen. 1985. *Hard Choices: How Women Decide about Work, Career, and Motherhood*. Berkeley: University of California Press.

——. 2009. "Changing Lives, Resistant Institutions: A New Generation Negotiates Gender, Work, and Family Change." *Sociological Forum* 24, no. 4 (December): 735–53. http://doi.org/10.1111/j.1573-7861.2009.01134.x.

Gerstel, Naomi. 1977. "The Feasibility of Commuter Marriage." In *The Family: Functions and Conflicts and Symbols*, edited by Peter J. Stein, Judith Richman, and Natalie Hannon, 357–67. Reading, MA: Addison Wesley.

——. 1978. "Commuter Marriage." PhD. diss., Columbia University.

Gerstel, Naomi, and Harriet Engel Gross. 1982. "Commuter Marriages: A Review." *Marriage & Family Review* 5, no. 2: 71–93. https://doi.org/10.1300/J002v05n02_05.

Gerstel, Naomi, and Harriet Engel Gross. 1984. *Commuter Marriage: A Study of Work and Family*. New York: Guilford Press.

Gibson-Davis, Christina M., Kathryn Edin, and Sara McLanahan. 2005. "High Hopes but Even Higher Expectations: The Retreat from Marriage among Low-Income Couples." *Journal of Marriage and Family* 67, no. 5 (December): 1301–12. http://doi.org/10.1111/j.1741-3737.2005.00218.x.

Giddens, Anthony. 1992. *The Transformation of Intimacy: Sexuality, Love and Eroticism in Modern Societies*. Stanford, CA: Stanford University Press.

Glaser, Barney G., and Anselm L. Strauss. 1967. *The Discovery of Grounded Theory: Strategies for Qualitative Research*. Chicago: Aldine.

Glotzer, Richard, and Anne Cairns Federlein. 2007. "Miles That Bind: Commuter Marriage and Family Strengths." *Michigan Family Review* 12, no. 1: 7–31. https://doi.org/10.3998/mfr.4919087.0012.102.

Goffman, Erving. 1959. *The Presentation of Self in Everyday Life*. New York: Anchor.

——. (1963) 2009. *Stigma: Notes on the Management of Spoiled Identity*. New York: Simon and Schuster.

Govaerts, Kathrijn, and David N. Dixon. 1988. ". . . Until Careers Do Us Part: Vocational and Marital Satisfaction in the Dual-Career Commuter Marriage." *International Journal for the Advancement of Counselling* 11, no. 4 (December): 265–81. https://doi.org/10.1007/BF00117685.

Gove, Walter R. 1973. "Sex, Marital Status and Mortality." *American Journal of Sociology* 79, no. 1 (July): 45–67. https://doi.org/10.1086/225505.

Grose, Jessica. 2011. "Does Absence Actually Make the Heart Grow Fonder?" *Slate*, September 23. http://www.slate.com/articles/double_x/doublex/2011/09/does_absence_actually_make_the_heart_grow_fonder.html.

Gross, Harriet Engel. 1980a. "Couples Who Live Apart: Time/Place Disjunctions and Their Consequences." *Symbolic Interaction* 3, no. 2 (Fall): 69–82. https://doi.org/10.1525/si.1980.3.2.69.

——. 1980b. "Dual-Career Couples Who Live Apart: Two Types." *Journal of Marriage and the Family* 42, no. 3 (August): 567–76. https://doi.org/10.2307/351900.

Gross, Neil, and Solon Simmons. 2002. "Intimacy as a Double-Edged Phenomenon? An Empirical Test of Giddens." *Social Forces* 81, no. 2 (December): 531–55. https://doi.org/10.1353/sof.2003.0011.

Groves, Melissa M., and Diane M. Horm-Wingerd. 1991. "Commuter Marriages: Personal, Family and Career Issues." *Sociology and Social Research* 75: 212–17.

Guldner, Gregory. 2003. *Long Distance Relationships: The Complete Guide*. Corona, CA: JF Milne.

Hall, David R. 1996. "Marriage as a Pure Relationship: Exploring the Link between Premarital Cohabitation and Divorce in Canada." *Journal of Comparative Family Studies* 27, no. 1 (Spring): 1–12. http://www.jstor.org/stable/41602429.

Hannaford, Dinah. 2017. *Marriage without Borders: Transnational Spouses in Neoliberal Senegal*. Philadelphia: University of Pennsylvania Press.

Harlan, Chico. 2016. "Ambition Enough for Two." *Washington Post*, January 29. http://www.washingtonpost.com/sf/national/2016/01/29/deciderscruz/.

Harrell, Margaret C. 2003. "Gender-and Class-Based Role Expectations for Army Spouses." In *Anthropology and the United States Military*, edited by Pamela R. Frese and Margaret C. Harrell, 69–94. New York: Palgrave Macmillan.

Harvey, Michael G. 1995. "The Impact of Dual-Career Families on International Relocations." *Human Resource Management Review* 5, no. 3 (Autumn): 223–44. https://doi.org/10.1016/1053-4822(95)90003-9.

——. 1998. "Dual-Career Couples during International Relocation: The Trailing Spouse." *International Journal of Human Resource Management* 9, no. 2: 309–33. https://doi.org/10.1080/095851998341116.

Harvey, Michael, and Danielle Wiese. 1998. "The Dual-Career Couple: Female Expatriates and Male Trailing Spouses." *Thunderbird International Business Review* 40, no. 4 (July/August): 359–88. https://doi.org/10.1002/tie.4270400404.

Haskey, John, and Jane Lewis. 2006. "Living-Apart-Together in Britain: Context and Meaning." *International Journal of Law in Context* 2, no. 1 (March): 37–48. https://doi.org/10.1017/S1744552306001030.

Herman-Kinney, Nancy J., and David A. Kinney. 2013. "Sober as Deviant: The Stigma of Sobriety and How Some College Students 'Stay Dry' on a 'Wet' Campus." *Journal of Contemporary Ethnography* 42, no. 1: 64–103. https://doi.org/10.1177/0891241612458954.

Heymann, Jody. 2000. *The Widening Gap: Why America's Working Families Are in Jeopardy and What Can Be Done about It*. New York: Basic Books.

Hill, Martha S., and W. Jean Yeung. 1999. "How Has the Changing Structure of Opportunities Affected Transitions to Adulthood?" In *Transitions to Adulthood in a Changing Economy*, edited by Alan Booth, Ann C. Crouter, and Michael J. Shanahan, 3–39. Westport, CT: Praeger.

Hiltz, Starr Roxanne, and Murray Turoff. (1978) 1993. *The Network Nation: Human Communication via Computer*. Cambridge, MA: MIT Press.

Hochschild, Arlie Russell. 1990. *The Second Shift*. New York: Avon.

——. 1997. *The Time Bind: When Work Becomes Home and Home Becomes Work*. New York: Metropolitan Books.

Holmes, Mary. 2004a. "An Equal Distance? Individualisation, Gender and Intimacy in Distance Relationships." *The Sociological Review* 52, no. 2 (May): 180–200. http://doi.org/10.1111/j.1467-954X.2004.00464.x.

——. 2004b. "The Precariousness of Choice in the New Sentimental Order: A Response to Bawin-Legros." *Current Sociology* 52, no. 2: 251–57. http://doi.org/10.1177/0011392104041811.

——. 2010. "The Loves of Others: Autoethnography and Reflexivity in Researching Distance Relationships." *Qualitative Sociology Review* 6, no. 2 (August): 89–104. http://www.qualitativesociologyreview.org/ENG/Volume16/QSR_6_2_Holmes.pdf.

——. 2014. *Distance Relationships: Intimacy and Emotions amongst Academics and Their Partners in Dual-Locations*. Basingstoke: Palgrave Macmillan.

Holmes, Seth. 2013. *Fresh Fruit, Broken Bodies: Migrant Farmworkers in the United States*. Berkeley: University of California Press.

Holt, Paula A., and Gerald L. Stone. 1988. "Needs, Coping Strategies, and Coping Outcomes Associated with Long-Distance Relationships." *Journal of College Student Development*. 29, no. 2: 136–41.

Humphreys, Laud. 2009 [1975]. *Tearoom Trade, Enlarged Edition: Impersonal Sex in Public Places*. New Brunswick, NJ: Transaction Publishers.

Innstrand, Siw Tone, Ellen Melbye Langballe, Erik Falkum, Geir Arild Espnes, and Olaf Gjerløw Aasland. 2009. "Gender-Specific Perceptions of Four Dimensions of the Work/Family Interaction." *Journal of Career Assessment*. 17, no. 4 (2009): 402–16. https://doi.org/10.1177/1069072709334238.

Isidore, Chris. 2017. "IBM Tells Employees Working at Home to Get Back to the Office." *CNN*. May 19. http://money.cnn.com/2017/05/19/technology/ibm-work-at-home/index.html.

Jackson, Anita P., Ronald P. Brown, and Karen E. Patterson-Stewart. 2000. "African Americans in Dual-Career Commuter Marriages: An Investigation of Their Experiences." *The Family Journal* 8, no. 1: 22–36. https://doi.org/10.1177/1066480700081005.

Jamieson, Lynn. 1999. "Intimacy Transformed? A Critical Look at the Pure Relationship." *Sociology* 33, no. 3: 477–94. https://is.muni.cz/el/1423/podzim2011/SOC402/um/JAMIESON_Intimacy_Transformed.pdf.

Johnson, Sharon Ervin. 1987. "Weaving the Threads: Equalizing Professional and Personal Demands Faced by Commuting Career Couples." *Journal of the National Association of Women Deans, Administrators, and Counselors* 50, no. 2: 3–10.

Kiesler, Sara, Jane Siegel, and Timothy W. McGuire. 1984. "Social Psychological Aspects of Computer-Mediated Communication." *American Psychologist* 39, no. 10: 1123–34. https://doi.org/10.1037/0003-066X.39.10.1123.

Kirschner, Betty Frankle, and Laurel Richardson Walum. 1978. "Two-Location Families." *Journal of Family and Economic Issues* 1, no. 4 (November): 513–25. https://doi.org/10.1007/BF01083436.

Klinenberg, Eric. 2012. *Going Solo: The Extraordinary Rise and Surprising Appeal of Living Alone.* New York: Penguin.

Knobloch, Leanne K., and Jennifer A. Theiss. 2012. "Experiences of U.S. Military Couples During the Post-Deployment Transition: Applying the Relational Turbulence Model." *Journal of Social and Personal Relationships* 29, no. 4: 423–50. https://doi.org/10.1177/0265407511431186.

Kolozsvari, Orsolya. 2015. " 'Physically We Are Apart, Mentally We Are Not.' Creating a Shared Space and a Sense of Belonging in Long-Distance Relationships." *Qualitative Sociology Review* 11, no. 4: 102–15.

Kruger, Justin, Nicholas Epley, Jason Parker, and Zhi-Wen Ng. 2005. "Egocentrism Over E-mail: Can We Communicate As Well As We Think?" *Journal of Personality and Social Psychology* 89, no. 6: 925–36. https://doi.org/10.1037/0022-3514.89.6.925.

Langton, Lynn, and Nicole Leeper Piquero. 2007. "Can General Strain Theory Explain White- Collar Crime? A Preliminary Investigation of the Relationship between Strain and Select White-Collar Offenses." *Journal of Criminal Justice* 35, no. 1: 1–15. https://doi.org/10.1016/j.jcrimjus.2006.11.011.

Lauer, Sean R., and Carrie Yodanis. 2011. "Individualized Marriage and the Integration of Resources." *Journal of Marriage and Family* 73, no. 3 (June): 669–83. https://doi.org/10.1111/j.1741-3737.2011.00836.x.

Laumann, Edward O., John H. Gagnon, Robert T. Michael, and Stuart Michaels. 1994. *The Social Organization of Sexuality: Sexual Practices in the United States.* Chicago: University of Chicago Press.

Lefebvre, Henri. (1991) 2014. "The Production of Space." In *The People, Place, and Space Reader*, edited by Jen Jack Gieseking, William Mangold, Cindi Katz, Setha Low, and Susan Saegert, 289–93. New York: Routledge.

Levin, Irene. 2004. "Living Apart Together: A New Family Form." *Current Sociology* 52, no. 2: 223-40. https://doi.org/10.1177/0011392104041809.

Levin, Irene, and Jan Trost. 1999. "Living Apart Together." *Community, Work & Family* 2, no. 3: 279–94. https://doi.org/10.1080/13668809908412186.

Li, Shu-Chu Sarrina. 2007. "Computer-Mediated Communication and Group Decision Making." *Small Group Research* 38, no. 5: 593–614. https://doi.org/10.1177/1046496407304335.

Liazos, Alexander. 1972. "The Poverty of the Sociology of Deviance: Nuts, Sluts, and 'Preverts.' " *Social Problems* 20, no. 1 (Summer): 103–20. https://doi.org/10.2307/799504.

Licoppe, Christian. 2004. " 'Connected' Presence: The Emergence of a New Repertoire for Managing Social Relationships in a Changing Communication Technoscape." *Environment and Planning D: Society and Space* 22, no. 1: 135–56. https://doi.org/10.1068/d323t.

Light, Audrey. 2004. "Gender Differences in the Marriage and Cohabitation Income Premium." *Demography* 41, no. 2 (May): 263–84. https://doi.org/10.1353/dem.2004.0016.

Lindemann, Danielle J. 2012. *Dominatrix: Gender, Eroticism, and Control in the Dungeon.* Chicago: University of Chicago Press.

———. 2017a. "Commuter Spouses and the Changing American Family." *Contexts* 16, no. 4: 26–31. https://doi.org/10.1177/1536504217742388.

———. 2017b. "Going the Distance: Individualism and Interdependence in the Commuter Marriage." *Journal of Marriage and Family* 79, no. 5 (October): 1419–34. https://doi.org/10.1111/jomf.12408.

———. 2017c. "'Doing and Undoing Gender in Commuter Marriages." *Sex Roles* (October 23): 1–14. https://doi.org/10.1007/s11199-017-0852-x.

Lindemann, Danielle J., and Steven J. Tepper. 2012. *Painting with Broader Strokes: Reassessing the Value of an Arts Degree.* Bloomington, IN: Strategic National Arts Alumni Project. http://snaap.indiana.edu/pdf/SNAAP_Special%20Report_1.pdf.

Lindemann, Danielle J., Steven J. Tepper, and Heather Laine Talley. 2017. "'I Don't Take My Tuba to Work at Microsoft': Arts Graduates and the Portability of Creative Identity." *American Behavioral Scientist* 61, no. 12: 1555–78. https://doi.org/10.1177/0002764217734276.

Linehan, Margaret, and James S. Walsh. 2001. "Key Issues in the Senior Female International Career Move: A Qualitative Study in a European Context." *British Journal of Management* 12, no. 1 (March): 85–95. https://doi.org/10.1111/1467-8551.00187.

Livingston, Beth A. 2014. "Bargaining Behind the Scenes: Spousal Negotiation, Labor, and Work—Family Burnout." *Journal of Management* 40, no. 4: 949–77. https://doi.org/10.1177/0149206311428355.

Livingston, Gretchen. 2015. "For Most Highly Educated Women, Motherhood Doesn't Start Until the 30's." Pew Research Center. January 15. http://www.pewresearch.org/fact-tank/2015/01/15/for-most-highly-educated-women-motherhood-doesnt-start-until-the-30s/

Lopez, Mark Hugo, and Ana Gonzalez-Barrera. 2014. "Women's College Enrollment Gains Leave Men Behind." Pew Research Center. March 6. http://www.pewresearch.org/fact-tank/2014/03/06/womens-college-enrollment-gains-leave-men-behind/.

Lorber, Judith. 1994. *Paradoxes of Gender.* New Haven, CT: Yale University Press.

Lundberg, Shelly, and Elaina Rose. 2000. "Parenthood and the Earnings of Married Men and Women." *Labour Economics* 7, no. 6: 689–710. https://doi.org/10.1016/S0927-5371(00)00020-8.

Lynch, James J. 1977. *The Broken Heart: The Medical Consequences of Loneliness.* New York: Basic Books.

Lyssens-Danneboom, Vicky, and Dimitri Mortelmans. 2014. "Living Apart Together and Money: New Partnerships, Traditional Gender Roles." *Journal of Marriage and Family* 76, no. 5 (October): 949–66. https://doi.org/10.1111/jomf.12136.

Magnuson, Sandy, and Ken Norem. 1999. "Challenges for Higher Education Couples in Commuter Marriages: Insights for Couples and Counselors Who Work with Them." *The Family Journal* 7, no. 2: 125–34. https://doi.org/10.1177/1066480799072005.

Mallen, Michael J., Susan X. Day, and Melinda A. Green. 2003. "Online Versus Face-to-Face Conversation: An Examination of Relational and Discourse Variables." *Psychotherapy: Theory, Research, Practice, Training* 40, nos. 1–2 (Spring–Summer): 155–163. https://doi.org/10.1037/0033-3204.40.1/2.155.

Mattingly, Marybeth J., and Suzanne M. Bianchi. 2003. "Gender Differences in the Quantity and Quality of Free Time: The U.S. Experience." *Social Forces* 81, no. 3 (March): 999–1030. https://doi.org/10.1353/sof.2003.0036.

Mcbride, M. Chad, and Karla Mason Bergen. 2014. "Voices of Women in Commuter Marriages: A Site of Discursive Struggle." *Journal of Social and Personal Relationships* 31, no. 4: 554–72. https://doi.org/10.1177/0265407514522890.

McFall, Brooke Helppie, and Marta Murray-Close. 2016. "Moving Out to Move Up: Dual- Career Migration and Work–Family Tradeoffs." *Economic Inquiry* 54, no. 1 (January): 44–62. https://doi.org/10.1111/ecin.12283.

McNulty, Yvonne. 2012. " 'Being Dumped in to Sink or Swim': An Empirical Study of Organizational Support for the Trailing Spouse." *Human Resource Development International* 15, no. 4: 417–34. https://doi.org/10.1080/13678868.2012.721985.

Mennino, Sue Falter, Beth A. Rubin, and April Brayfield. 2005. "Home-to-Job and Job-to-Home Spillover: The Impact of Company Policies and Workplace Culture." *The Sociological Quarterly* 46, no. 2: 107–35. https://doi.org/10.1111/j.1533-8525.2005.00006.x.

Merton, Robert. 1938. "Social Structure and Anomie." *American Sociological Review* 3, no. 5 (October): 672-82. http://www.jstor.org/stable/2084686.

——. 1968. *Social Theory and Social Structure*. New York: Free Press.

Messner, Steven, and Richard Rosenfeld. 1994. *Crime and the American Dream*. Belmont, CA: Cengage Learning.

Milan, Anne and Alice Peters. 2003. "Couples Living Apart." *Canadian Social Trends* (summer). Statistics Canada—Catalogue No. 11–008. http://www.statcan.gc.ca/pub/11-008-x/2003001/article/6552-eng.pdf.

Milkie, Melissa A., Sara B. Raley, and Suzanne M. Bianchi. 2009. "Taking on the Second Shift: Time Allocations and Time Pressures of U.S. Parents with Preschoolers." *Social Forces* 88, no. 2 (December): 487–517. https://doi.org/10.1353/sof.0.0268.

Mills, C. Wright. 2000. *The Sociological Imagination*. New York: Oxford University Press.

Morrison, Rachel L. 2009. "Are Women Tending and Befriending in the Workplace? Gender Differences in the Relationship between Workplace Friendships and Organizational Outcomes." *Sex Roles* 60, no. 1 (January): 1–13. https://doi.org/10.1007/s11199-008-9513-4.

Murray-Close, Marta. 2013. "Living Far Apart Together: Dual-Career Location Constraints and Marital Non-Cohabitation." Paper presented at Proceedings of the Population Association of America, New Orleans, Louisiana, April 11–13.

National Alliance for Caregiving and AARP. 2009. *Caregiving in the U.S., 2009*. Bethesda, MD: National Alliance for Caregiving. http://www.caregiving.org/data/Caregiving_in_the_US_2009_full_report.pdf.

National Center for Education Statistics. 2012. "Fast Facts: Degrees Conferred by Sex and Race." http://nces.ed.gov/fastfacts/display.asp?id=72.

Neustaedter, Carman, and Saul Greenberg. 2012. "Intimacy in Long-Distance Relationships over Video Chat." *Proceedings of the SIGCHI Conference on Human Factors in Computing Systems*, 753–62. http://summit.sfu.ca/system/files/iritems1/10361/2011-IntimateMediaSpaces.Report2011-1014-26.pdf.

Neustatter, Angela. 2013. "Divided We Stand: Committed Couples Who Live Apart." *The Telegraph*, April 22. http://www.telegraph.co.uk/women/sex/relationship-advice-and-romance/10003381/Divided-we-stand-committed-couples-who-live-apart.html.

Newby, John H., James E. McCarroll, Robert J. Ursano, Zizhong Fan, Jun Shigemura, and Yvonne Tucker-Harris. 2005. "Positive and Negative Consequences of a Military Deployment." *Military Medicine* 170, no. 10 (October): 815–19. https://doi.org/10.7205/MILMED.170.10.815.

Nippert-Eng, Christena. 1996. "Calendars and Keys: The Classification of 'Home' and 'Work.'" *Sociological Forum* 11, no. 3: 563–82. https://doi.org10.1007/BF02408393.

Odum, Howard W. 1937. "Notes on the Technicways in Contemporary Society." *American Sociological Review* 2, no. 3 (June): 336–46. http://www.jstor.org/stable/2084865.

——. "Folk Sociology as a Subject Field for the Historical Study of Total Human Society and the Empirical Study of Group Behavior." *Social Forces* 31, no. 3 (March): 193–223. http://www.jstor.org/stable/2574217.

Ozawa, Martha N., and Hong-Sik Yoon. 2002. "The Economic Benefit of Remarriage: Gender and Income Class." *Journal of Divorce & Remarriage* 36, nos. 3–4: 21–39. https://doi.org/10.1300/J087v36n03_02.

Papanek, Hanna. 1973. "Men, Women, and Work: Reflections on the Two-Person Career." *American Journal of Sociology* 78, no. 4 (January): 852–72. https://doi.org/10.1086/225406.

Parreñas, Rhacel Salazar. 2001. *Servants of Globalization: Women, Migration, and Domestic Work*. Stanford, CA: Stanford University Press.

Passas, Nikos. 1990. "Anomie and Corporate Deviance." *Contemporary Crises* 14, no. 2: 157–78. https://doi.org/10.1007/BF00728269.

Pemberton, David. 2015. "Statistical Definition of 'Family' Unchanged Since 1930." United States Census Blog. January 28. https://www.census.gov/newsroom/blogs/random-samplings/2015/01/statistical-definition-of-family-unchanged-since-1930.html.

Pew Research Center. 2010. *The Decline of Marriage and Rise of New Families*. Pew Research Center. http://www.pewsocialtrends.org/files/2010/11/pew-social-trends-2010-families.pdf.

Phillips, Gerald M., and Gerald M. Santoro. 1989. "Teaching Group Discussion via Computer-Mediated Communication." *Communication Education* 38, no. 2: 151–61. https://doi.org/10.1080/03634528909378748.

Pini, Barbara, and Robyn Mayes. 2012. "Gender, Emotions and Fly-in Fly-out Work." *Australian Journal of Social Issues* 47, no. 1 (March): 71–86. https://doi.org/10.1002/j.1839-4655.2012.tb00235.x.

Pullen, Alison, and David Knights. 2007. "Editorial: Undoing Gender: Organizing and Disorganizing Performance." *Gender, Work & Organization* 14, no. 6 (November): 505–11. https://doi.org/10.1111/j.1468-0432.2007.00368.x.

Putnam, Robert D. 2000. *Bowling Alone: The Collapse and Revival of American Community*. New York: Simon and Schuster.

Radloff, Lenore. 1975. "Sex Differences in Depression" *Sex Roles* 1, no. 3 (September): 249–65. https://doi.org/10.1007/BF00287373.

Raley, Sara, Suzanne M. Bianchi, and Wendy Wang. 2012. "When Do Fathers Care? Mothers' Economic Contribution and Fathers' Involvement in Child Care." *American Journal of Sociology* 117, no. 5 (March): 1422–59. https://doi.org/10.1086/663354.

Reed-Danahay, Deborah. 2001. "Autobiography, Intimacy and Ethnography." In *Handbook of Ethnography*, edited by Paul Atkinson, 407–25. London: Sage.

Rhodes, Angel R. 2002. "Long-Distance Relationships in Dual-Career Commuter Couples: A Review of Counseling Issues." *The Family Journal* 10, no. 4: 398–404. https://doi.org/10.1177/106648002236758.

Rindfuss, Ronald R., and Elizabeth Hervey Stephen. 1990. "Marital Noncohabitation: Separation Does Not Make the Heart Grow Fonder." *Journal of Marriage and the Family* 52, no. 1 (February): 259–70. https://doi.org/10.2307/352856.

Risman, Barbara J. 1998. *Gender Vertigo*. New Haven, CT: Yale University Press.

———. 2009. "From Doing to Undoing: Gender as We Know It." *Gender & Society* 23, no. 1: 81–84. https://doi.org/10.1177/0891243208326874.

Robinson, Matthew, and Daniel Murphy. 2009. *Greed Is Good: Maximization and Elite Deviance in America*. Lanham, MD: Rowman & Littlefield.

Rosenblum, Constance. 2013. "Living Apart Together." *New York Times*, September 13. http://www.nytimes.com/2013/09/15/realestate/living-apart-together.html?pagewanted=all&_r=2&.

Roseneil, Sasha. 2006. "On Not Living with a Partner: Unpicking Coupledom and Cohabitation." *Sociological Research Online* 11, no. 3. http://www.socresonline.org.uk/11/3/roseneil.html.

Rotter, Joseph C., Donald E. Barnett, and Mary L. Fawcett. 1998. "On the Road Again: Dual- Career Commuter Relationships." *The Family Journal* 6, no. 1: 46–48. https://doi.org/10.1177/1066480798061009.

Rubington, Earl. 1973. *Alcohol Problems and Social Control*. Columbus, OH: Merrill.

Sayer, Liana C. 2005. "Gender, Time and Inequality: Trends in Women's and Men's Paid Work, Unpaid Work and Free Time." *Social Forces* 84, no. 1 (September): 285–303. https://doi.org/10.1353/sof.2005.0126.

Schoen, Robert, and James R. Kluegel. 1988. "The Widening Gap in Black and White Marriage Rates: The Impact of Population Composition and Differential Marriage Propensities." *American Sociological Review* 53, no. 6 (December): 895–907. www.jstor.org/stable/2095898.

Schur, Edwin M. 1971. *Labeling Deviant Behavior: Its Sociological Implications*. New York: Harper & Row.

Scott, Andrea Towers. 2002. ""Communication Characterizing Successful Long Distance Marriages." PhD diss., Louisiana State University.

Sennett, Richard. 1998. *The Corrosion of Character: The Personal Consequences of Work in the New Capitalism*. New York: W. W. Norton & Company.

Shahnasarian, Michael. 1991. "Job Relocation and the Trailing Spouse." *Journal of Career Development* 17, no. 3 (March): 179–84. https:\\doi.org\10.1007/BF01322025.

Sharp, Susan F., Toni L. Terling-Watt, Leslie A. Atkins, Jay Trace Gilliam, and Anna Sanders. "Purging Behavior in a Sample of College Females: A Research Note on General Strain Theory and Female Deviance." *Deviant Behavior* 22, no. 2: 171–88. https://doi.org/10.1080/016396201750065036.

Shaw, Susan M. 2001. "Conceptualizing Resistance: Women's Leisure as Political Practice." *Journal of Leisure Research* 33, no. 2: 186–201. http://www.nrpa.org/globalassets/journals/jlr/2001/volume-33/jlr-volume-33-number-2-pp-186-201.pdf

Shuy, Roger W. 2003. "In-Person versus Telephone Interviewing." In *Inside Interviewing: New Lenses, New Concerns*, edited by James Holstein and Jaber F. Gubrium, 175–93. Thousand Oaks, CA: Sage.

Simon, David R., and D. Stanley Eitzen. 2002. *Elite Deviance*. Boston: Allyn and Bacon.

Simon, Robin W. 2002. "Revisiting the Relationships among Gender, Marital Status, and Mental Health." *American Journal of Sociology* 107, no. 4 (January): 1065–96. https://doi.org/10.1086/339225.

Smart, Carol, and Beccy Shipman. 2004. "Visions in Monochrome: Families, Marriage and the Individualization Thesis." *The British Journal of Sociology* 55, no. 4 (December): 491–509. https://doi.org/10.1111/j.1468-4446.2004.00034.x.

Smock, Pamela J., Wendy D. Manning, and Meredith Porter. 2005. " 'Everything's There Except Money': How Money Shapes Decisions to Marry among Cohabitors." *Journal of Marriage and Family* 67, no. 3 (August): 680–96. http://doi.org/10.1111/j.1741-3737.2005.00162.x.

Soja, Edward W. 1989. *Postmodern Geographies: The Reassertion of Space in Critical Social Theory*. New York: Verso.

Stacey, Judith. 2012. *Unhitched: Love, Marriage, and Family Values from West Hollywood to Western China*. New York: New York University Press.

Stack, Steven, and J. Ross Eshleman. 1998. "Marital Status and Happiness: A 17-Nation Study." *Journal of Marriage and the Family* 60, no. 2 (May): 527–36. https://doi.org/10.2307/353867.

Stafford, Laura. 2005. *Maintaining Long-Distance and Cross-Residential Relationships*. Mahwah, NJ: Erlbaum.

Stafford, Laura and James R. Reske. 1990. "Idealization and Communication in Long-Distance Premarital Relationships." *Family Relations* 39, no. 3 (July): 274–79. https://doi.org/10.2307/584871.

Stone, Katherine V.W., and Harry Arthurs, eds. 2013. *Rethinking Workplace Regulation: Beyond the Standard Contract of Employment*. New York: Russell Sage Foundation.

Stone, Pamela. 2007. *Opting Out?: Why Women Really Quit Careers and Head Home*. Berkeley: University of California Press.

Sullivan, Oriel. 2004. "Changing Gender Practices within the Household: A Theoretical Perspective." *Gender & Society* 18, no. 2: 207–22. https://doi.org/10.1177/0891243203261571.

——. 2011. "An End to Gender Display Through the Performance of Housework? A Review and Reassessment of the Quantitative Literature Using Insights from the Qualitative Literature." *Journal of Family Theory and Review* 3, no. 1 (March): 1–13. httos://doi.org/10.1111/j.1756-2589.2010.00074.x.

Sullivan, Oriel, and Jonathan Gershuny. 2001. "Cross-National Changes in Time-use: Some Sociological (Hi)stories Re-examined." *British Journal of Sociology* 52, no. 2 (June): 331-47. https://doi.org/10.1080/00071310120045015.

Swanbrow, Diane. 2008. "Exactly How Much Housework Does a Husband Create?" *Michigan News*. April 3. http://ns.umich.edu/new/releases/6452.

Swidler, Ann. 2013. *Talk of Love: How Culture Matters*. Chicago: University of Chicago Press.

Tessina, Tina B. 2008. *The Commuter Marriage: Keep Your Relationship Close While You're Far Apart*. Avon, MA: Adams Media.

Theiss, Jennifer A., and Leanne K. Knobloch. 2015⁴. "Relational Turbulence and the Post- Deployment Transition: Self, Partner, and Relationship Focused Turbulence." *Communication Research* 41, no. 1: 27–51. https://doi.org/10.1177/00936 50211429285.

Thomas, W. I., and Dorothy Swaine Thomas. 1928. *The Child in America: Behavior Problems and Programs*. New York: Knopf.

Thompson, Linda, and Alexis J. Walker. 1989. "Gender in Families: Women and Men in Marriage, Work, and Parenthood." *Journal of Marriage and the Family* 51, no. 4 (November): 845–71. https://doi.org/10.2307/353201.

Thornton, Arland, and Linda Young-DeMarco. 2001. "Four Decades of Trends in Attitudes toward Family Issues in the United States: The 1960s through the 1990s." *Journal of Marriage and Family* 63, no. 4 (November): 1009–37. https://doi.org/10.1111/j.1741-3737.2001.01009.x.

Tkaczyk, Christopher. 2013. "Marissa Mayer Breaks Her Silence on Yahoo's Telecommuting Policy." *Fortune*, April 19. http://fortune.com/2013/04/19/marissa-mayer-breaks-her-silence-on-yahoos-telecommuting-policy/.

United States Bureau of Labor Statistics. 2008. "Table 1. Time Spent in Primary Activities (1) and the Percent of Married Mothers and Fathers Who Did the Activities on an Average Day by Employment Status and Age of Youngest Own Household Child, Average for the Combined Years 2003–06." Accessed July 8. http://www.bls.gov/news.release/atus2.t01.htm.

United States Census Bureau. 2012. "Statistical Abstract of the United States: 2012." http://www.census.gov/prod/2011pubs/12statab/labor.pdf.

Van der Klis, Marjolijn, and Clara H. Mulder. 2008. "Beyond the Trailing Spouse: The Commuter Partnership as an Alternative to Family Migration." *Journal of Housing and the Built Environment* 23, no. 1 (March): 1–19. https://doi.org/10.1007/s10901-007-9096-3.

Wade, Lisa. 2016. "The Invisible Workload That Drags Women Down." *Money*, December 29. https://time.com/money/4561314/women-work-home-gender-gap/.

——. 2017. "The Modern Marriage Trap—and What to Do About It." *Money*, January 11. https://time.com/money/4630251/the-modern-marriage-trap-and-what-to-do-about-it/.

Waldfogel, Jane. 1997. "The Effect of Children on Women's Wages." *American Sociological Review* 62, no. 2 (April): 209–17. www.jstor.org/stable/2657300.

Walther, Joseph B. 1996. "Computer-Mediated Communication: Impersonal, Interpersonal, and Hyperpersonal Interaction." *Communication Research* 23, no. 1: 3–43. http://doi.org/10.1177/009365096023001001.

——. 2007. "Selective Self-Presentation in Computer-Mediated Communication: Hyperpersonal Dimensions of Technology, Language, and Cognition." *Computers in Human Behavior* 23, no. 5 (September): 2538–57. https://doi.org/10.1016/j.chb. 2006.05.002.

Wang, Wendy, and Kim Parker. 2014. *Record Share of Americas Have Never Married as Values, Economics and Gender Patterns Change*. Washington, DC: Pew Research Center's Social and Demographics Trends project. September. http://www.pewsocial trends.org/2014/09/24/record-share-of-americans-have-never-married/.

Wang, Wendy, Kim Parker, and Paul Taylor. 2013. *Breadwinner Moms: Mothers Are the Sole or Primary Provider in Four-in-Ten Households with Children; Public Conflicted about the Growing Trend*. Washington, DC: Pew Research Center. http:// www.pewsocialtrends.org/2013/05/29/breadwinner-moms/.

West, Candace, and Don H. Zimmerman. 1987. "Doing Gender." *Gender & Society* 1, no. 2: 125–51. https://doi.org/10.1177/0891243287001002002.

West, Candace, and Don H. Zimmerman. 2009. "Accounting for Doing Gender." *Gender & Society* 23, no. 1: 112–22. https://doi.org/10.1177/0891243208326529.

Weston, Kath. 1997. *Families We Choose: Lesbians, Gays, Kinship*. New York: Columbia University Press.

Wilding, Raelene. 2006. "'Virtual' Intimacies? Families Communicating across Transnational Contexts." *Global Networks* 6, no. 2 (April): 125–42. https://doi. org/10.1111/j.1471-0374.2006.00137.x.

Williams, Kristi. 2003. "Has the Future of Marriage Arrived? A Contemporary Examination of Gender, Marriage, and Psychological Well-Being." *Journal of Health and Social Behavior* 44, no. 4: 470–87. https://www.ncbi.nlm.nih.gov/pmc/articles/ PMC4018193/.

Wilson, William Julius. 1987. *The Truly Disadvantaged: The Inner City, the Underclass, and Public Policy*. Chicago: University of Chicago Press.

Winfield, Fairlee E. 1985. *Commuter Marriage: Living Together, Apart*. New York: Columbia University Press.

Wolf-Wendel, Lisa E., Susan Twombly, and Suzanne Rice. 2000. "Dual-Career Couples: Keeping Them Together." *Journal of Higher Education* 71, no. 3: 291–321. https:// doi.org/10.1080/00221546.2000.11780824.

Woolstenhulme, Jared L., Benjamin W. Cowan, Jill J. McCluskey, and Tori C. Byington. 2012. "Evaluating the Two-Body Problem: Measuring Joint Hire Productivity within a University." October 10. http://ses.wsu.edu/wp-content/uploads/2014/09/ JaredW.pdf.

Young, Cathy. 2014. "What Women Still Want in a Husband." *Newsday*, editorial, September 30. https://www.newsday.com/opinion/columnists/cathy-young/what-women-still-want-in-a-husband-cathy-young-1.9437289.

Zippel, Kathrin. 2017. *Women in Global Science: Advancing Academic Careers through International Collaboration*. Stanford, CA: Stanford University Press.

Zvonkovic, Anisa M., Catherine Richards Solomon, Áine M. Humble, and Margaret Manoogian. 2005. "Family Work and Relationships: Lessons from Families of Men Whose Jobs Require Travel." *Family Relations* 54, no. 3 (July): 411–22. httos://doi. org/10.1111/j.1741-3729.2005.00327.x.

Index

academia
  and acceptability of commuter
    marriage, 60–65, 111, 160n3
  flexibility within, 121
  job market within, 4, 64, 71, 126, 135,
    157n2
  oversampling from, 10, 146
  spousal hiring within, 135
Acker, Joan, 82, 89, 115, 129, 131
apart togetherness, 17, 24–27, 31, 36,
    158n4
  See also LAT relationships
autoethnography, 13–14

Beck, Ulrich, 5
Beck-Gernsheim, Elisabeth, 5
Bergen, Karla Mason, 62, 158n11,
    161n3
Blair-Loy, Mary, 70–71, 129, 133
Butler, Judith, 82

Cairncross, Frances, 41–42, 55
Callero, Peter, 71
Cancian, Francesca, 137
Carter, Julia, 30–31
Cherlin, Andrew, 18–22, 24
children
  caretaking of, 12, 19, 50–53, 79,
    89–91, 104
  relationships with, 37, 122
  well-being of, 51–53, 115, 122, 137
  See also gender: and childcare
choice
  to live apart, 8, 11–12, 45, 59, 66–77,
    160n5
  within marriage, 3, 4, 19
cohabitation, 19, 21, 102, 113
  and communication, 26
  of commuter spouses, 65, 86, 93, 100,
    102, 108, 112
  See also reunification

collectivism, 72
communication, 6, 11, 114, 159n7
  and advantages of living apart, 25–26,
    35–36, 158n5
communication technologies
  benefits of, 38–39, 43–45, 55–56, 117
  inadequacies of, 11, 46–48, 55–56,
    108–9, 117, 123
  See also: forms of communication
commuter marriage
  definition of, 7, 143–4, 157n4
  origins of, 3
  prevalence of, 8–9, 62, 72, 157n1,
    158n5
conflict, 47–48, 119, 120
Coombs, Robert, 101
Coontz, Stephanie, 8, 18, 134, 158n1
Cruz, Heidi, 2, 50

Decision-making. *See* choice
deviance, 11, 59–64, 67–68, 75–76, 129,
  132, 160n1
divorce, 29, 55, 100–101, 136, 158n1
  among commuter spouses, 28, 65, 119,
    121, 145, 158n10
Durkheim, Emile, 101

elder care, 91

FaceTime, 34–35, 39, 44, 50, 56–57,
  114
Family
  census definition of, 62, 160n2
  structure of, 67, 76–77, 133, 136
FIFO spouses, 9, 54, 63
finances, 17, 18, 23, 74, 98–99, 102, 130
  and motivation for living apart, 8, 11,
    58–59, 65–70, 72–75, 161n10
  and negative impact of commuting,
    68–69, 117
forms of communication
  email, 39–40, 42–43, 159n4
  internet, 38–41, 43
  phone, 34, 38–39, 42–43, 46–47
  texting, 26, 39, 41, 44

video chatting, 39, 56–57, 117, 159n1.
  See also FaceTime

gender
  and childcare, 80, 83, 89–91, 99, 104,
    121–122, 136–137
  and education, 3–4
  and emotional labor, 101, 104–6,
    113–14
  and envy of commuter spouses, 99,
    108–111
  and friendship, 105–7, 113–14
  and health, 106, 138
  and housework, 81–84, 87–88,
    92–94, 97, 161n5
  and leisure time, 103–5, 110–11, 114
  and loneliness, 106–7, 112, 131
  and mobility decisions, 84
  and satisfaction with commuter
    marriage, 95–96, 103–7, 110, 124
  and stigma of commuter marriage,
    62–63, 132, 161n3
  and work experiences, 3, 77, 83–84,
    88–89, 95–96
  and work/life integration, 12, 77, 80,
    82–87, 89
gender roles, 3–4, 62, 80, 94–97, 101,
  114, 131–133
Gerson, Kathleen, 21
Gerstel, Naomi
  on communication in commuter
    marriage, 44–45, 56, 158n5, 159n5
  on gender roles in commuter marriage,
    3, 95–96, 102–3
  on individualism, 20
Giddens, Anthony, 11, 19–20, 22, 30,
  33, 128, 158n2
Gross, Harriet Engel. *See* Gerstel, Naomi

Hannaford, Dinah, 118
happiness, 13, 101–2, 116–18, 120–22
health, 11, 48–50, 101, 106, 118, 138
Holmes, Mary, 19, 146, 159n17, 159n2,
  161n3
home, 11, 36–38, 130, 159n2

identity. *See* professional work: and
    identity
individualism
  in commuter marriage, 20–22, 29–30,
    48, 53, 114–115, 128–131
  in marriage, 3, 15, 18–19, 30, 33, 129–31
infidelity, 27–28, 159n13
interdependence, 20–25, 29–30, 38,
    43–44, 48, 72, 102

job markets, 3, 4, 64, 71–72, 126
jobs. *See* work

kids. *See* children

LAT relationships, 5, 95, 138, 158n4
Lefebvre, Henri, 36–37, 128
Levin, Irene, 95, 103
Licoppe, Christian, 41, 44
love, 18–19, 30–32, 139

marriage
  health benefits of, 101
  individualization of, 7, 10–11, 18, 22,
    29, 32, 130
  meaning of, 10–11
men. *See* gender
Merton, Robert, 67–68, 74–76, 129,
    160n6
migrants, 9, 54, 66, 75
military spouses, 7, 9, 54, 63, 118–19,
    143, 157
money. *See* finances
Morrison, Rachel, 107
Murray-Close, Marta, 8–9, 62, 71–72,
    84, 146, 158n4, 162n3

Passas, Nikos, 61, 68
pets, 91–92
Poehler, Amy, 2
professional necessity, 12, 59–61, 70–71,
    75–76, 133, 160n3
professional work
  and identity, 7, 12, 70–72, 75, 129,
    133, 138

meaning of, 9, 11, 70–72, 76, 124,
    132–3
research focus on, 8–10, 142, 144,
    157n4, 158n6
professors. *See* academia

race
  and domestic workers, 93–94
  and marriage rates, 20
  and privilege, 10, 12, 59, 75
  in the sample, 10, 144
reunification, 113, 118–20, 122, 132
Risman, Barbara, 84–85, 129, 161n1

Same-sex couples, 7, 9–10, 21, 32,
    137–8, 158n1
satellite relationships, 37, 92, 94, 106,
    130, 145
sex, 17, 19, 26–28, 46, 112, 120, 142
Shaw, Susan, 114
Slaughter, Anne-Marie, 52
Soja, Edward, 37
space, 11, 36–38, 45–47, 50, 57, 108–9,
    128
stigma, 31, 60–63, 96, 115, 132,
    160n3
  and gender. *See* gender: and stigma of
    commuter marriage
strain theory. *See* Merton, Robert
Swidler, Ann, 31–32

technology. *See* communication
    technologies
telecommuting, 133–4
trailing spouses, 4–5, 84, 94,
    161n2
truckers, 66

Wade, Lisa, 104–5
Walther, Joseph, 11, 40, 55
West, Candace, 81–82, 96
Wilding, Raelene, 33, 47–48, 54
Williams, Kristi, 101
Winfield, Fairlee, 62, 158n6, 159n13,
    160nn3–4, 161n2, 162n1

women. *See* gender
work
  in the contingent economy, 4, 15, 127, 132
  specialization of, 6, 9, 11–12, 71–72, 76–77, 135–6
  See also professional work

work/life integration, 12, 77, 131, 134–5, 139
  and gender. *See* gender: and work/life integration

Zimmerman, Don H. *See* West, Candace

CPSIA information can be obtained
at www.ICGtesting.com
Printed in the USA
LVHW021143100219
607031LV00003B/636

9 781501 731181